Physical Characteristics of the Great Pyrenees
(from the American Kennel Club breed standard)

Shoulders: The shoulders are well laid back, well muscled, and lie close to the body. The upper arm meets the shoulder blade at approximately a right angle. The upper arm angles backward from the point of the shoulder to the elbow and is never perpendicular to the ground.

Body: The chest is moderately broad. Back and loin are broad and strongly coupled with some tuck-up.

Hindquarters: The angulation of the hindquarters is similar in degree to that of the forequarters. Thighs—Strongly muscular upper thighs extend from the pelvis at right angles. The rear pastern (metatarsus) is of medium length and perpendicular to the ground as the dog stands naturally. The rear legs are of sufficient bone and muscle to provide a balance with the frame. Double dewclaws are located on each rear leg.

Size: The height at the withers ranges from 27 inches to 32 inches for dogs and from 25 inches to 29 inches for bitches. A 27 inch dog weighs about 100 pounds and a 25 inch bitch weighs about 85 pounds.

Tail: The tailbones are of sufficient length to reach the hock. The tail is well plumed, carried low in repose and may be carried over the back, "making the wheel," when aroused.

Feet: Rounded, close-cupped, well padded, toes well arched.

Color: White or white with markings of gray, badger, reddish brown, or varying shades of tan.

P9-CKX-985

Great Pyrenees

By Juliette Cunliffe

Contents

Training Your Great Pyrenees   89

Begin with the basics of training the puppy and adult dog. Learn the principles of house-training the Great Pyrenees, including the use of crates and basic scent instincts. Enter Puppy Kindergarten and introduce the pup to his collar and leash and progress to the basic commands. Find out about obedience classes and other activities.

Healthcare of Your Great Pyrenees   113

By Lowell Ackerman DVM, DACVD
Become your dog's healthcare advocate and a well-educated canine keeper. Select a skilled and able veterinarian. Discuss pet insurance, vaccinations and infectious diseases, the neuter/spay decision and a sensible, effective plan for parasite control, including fleas, ticks and worms.

Showing Your Great Pyrenees   141

Step into the center ring and find out about the world of showing pure-bred dogs. Here's how to get started in AKC shows, how they are organized and what's required for your dog to become a champion. Take a leap into the realms of obedience trials, agility, earthdog events and tracking tests.

Your Aging Great Pyrenees   149

Know when to consider your Great Pyrenees a senior and what special needs he will have. Learn the signs of aging in terms of physical and behavioral traits and what your vet can do to optimize your dog's golden years. Consider some advice about saying goodbye to your beloved pet.

Photography by Isabelle Français and Carol Ann Johnson, with additional photographs by

Paulette Braun, T.J. Calhoun, Alan and Sandy Carey, Carolina Biological Supply, David Dalton, Bill Jonas, Dr. Dennis Kunkel, Tam C. Nguyen, Phototake, Michael Trafford, Alice van Kempen and Jean Claude Revy.

Illustrations by Patricia Peters

The publisher wishes to thank Gale B. Armstrong, Giovanni & Roberta Lazzeri Cardini, Marie-Claude Couty, Rhonda Dalton, Raymond Ducrey, Mrs. Beryl Lordy, Rocco Muraca, Michéle Etienne Serclérat, Mrs. Janet Srodzinski and the rest of the owners of the dogs featured in this book.

KENNEL CLUB BOOKS: **GREAT PYRENEES**
ISBN: 1-59378-319-1

Copyright © 2004
Kennel Club Books, Inc., 308 Main Street, Allenhurst, NJ 07711 USA
Cover Design Patented: US 6,435,559 B2 • Printed in South Korea

HISTORY OF THE
GREAT PYRENEES

The Great Pyrenees is known by several different names, but all of these names are derived from the Pyrenean mountain range in the Basque country, lying between Spain and France. It is in this mountainous region that the breed has long been used as a guardian for flocks of sheep and goats, working on steep slopes, in dense undergrowth and open pasture. The breed was widely used in this manner until the late 19th century, when large predators were eliminated from the region.

In the breed's homeland, the Great Pyrenees was used to guard animals from bears and wolves, so it was important that this magnificent breed not only was of great size but also had strength and stamina. Temperament, too, was incredibly important. There could be no nervousness, and yet no amount of aggression could be permitted.

Large Pyrenean-type dogs can be traced back to well before the

birth of Christ, for fossil remains have been found dating back to the Bronze Age (1800–1000 BC). It is believed that large, primarily white guardian dogs, the early ancestors of the Pyrenean breed, migrated from Asia Minor into Europe, both by sea and by land. By sea, the Phoenician traders went from Cadiz northward through Spain and then into the Pyrenees; by land, the dogs moved westward with the Aryan migration into Europe, thus helping to establish various different breeds, each of which developed its own individual characteristics.

Nina Scott Langley's renowned painting (circa 1930) of a Great Pyrenees created interest in the breed outside the Basque country where stretch the Pyrenean Mountains.

Facing page: A creation of the Basques, the Great Pyrenees is a unique, magnificent dog who is known as le Chien de Montagne des Pyrénées in its homeland and as the Pyrenean Mountain Dog in the UK.

The Maremma Sheepdog, sometimes referred to as the Maremmano-Abruzzese, comes from the Abruzzi Mountains in Italy. The Maremma closely resembles the Pyrenean breed, but is somewhat smaller.

Among these were the Maremma, Hungarian Kuvasz, Komondor, Slovensky Cuvac, Polish Tatra Mountain Dog, Anatolian Shepherd Dog, Akbash and Pyrenean Mastiff, the latter clearly a close relation of the Great Pyrenees.

Once in Spain, the climatic conditions under which the Great Pyrenees developed were similar to those of its native land, and these dogs remained in isolated mountainous regions until the Medieval period. An interesting early reference to the breed is a sculptured bas-relief, found over the North Gate of Carcassone, which bears the royal arms of France.

From French writings of 1407 we learn that "Great Dogs of the Mountains" were used to guard the Chateau of Lourdes. Here they were regularly used as guards for the men making their rounds, and provision was even made for them in the sentry boxes. French King Louis XIV adopted the breed as the Royal Dog of France in 1675, and this caused the breed to be highly sought after by French nobility.

Already these dogs were recognized for their usefulness, for they had both a good sense of smell and exceptionally good eyesight. Whatever their use, be it as flock guardian, pack animal or messenger, one Great Pyrenees was considered to be equal to two men.

CANIS LUPUS
"Grandma, what big teeth you have!" The gray wolf, a familiar figure in fairy tales and legends, has had its reputation tarnished and its population pummeled over the centuries. Yet it is the descendants of this much-feared creature to which we open our homes and hearts. Our beloved dog, *Canis domesticus*, derives directly from the gray wolf, a highly social canine that lives in elaborately structured packs. In the wild, the gray wolf can range from 60 to 175 pounds, standing between 25 and 40 inches in height.

MOVEMENT TO THE AMERICAS
Pyrenean dogs traveled to Newfoundland with Basque fishermen in 1662. They went as companion animals, but also as guardians. In Newfoundland, the Curly-Coated Retriever was already a favorite of English settlers in that land. The Pyreneans mated with these dogs, bringing about the Landseer Newfoundland, which is a large black and white dog.

THE NINETEENTH CENTURY
Britain's Queen Victoria, a well-known dog lover who did so much to draw attention to the breeds of dog she owned, had a

Great Pyrenees in 1850. By the mid-1880s, the breed was registered with the English Kennel Club and was shown at London's Crystal Palace. In France, the breed had been exhibited in the Zoological Gardens of the Bois de Bologne, on the outskirts of Paris, in 1863.

In 1897, Count H. A. Graff van Bylandt included the breed in his encyclopaedia, *Les Races de Chiens*, published in Brussels. In this, and in the 1904 edition, there were photographs of this majestic breed, hitherto unknown

MAIDA'S PATER

In the past, the Great Pyrenees was frequently used when an outcross was needed to infuse new blood to strengthen some of the larger breeds. Although Sir Walter Scott's famous dog Maida is always referred to as a Deerhound, his sire was actually a Great Pyrenees.

to so many dog fanciers, and the result was a sudden demand for puppies. However, in France, this did not have a positive effect on

The Pyrenean Shepherd Dog (called the Berger des Pyrenees in France) has worked in association with the Great Pyrenees for many generations in the Basque country. This smaller breed herds the flock, while the Great Pyrenees guards from human and lupine marauders.

The Hungarian Komondor belongs to the family of large white flock guardians. The breed is distinctive for its completely corded coat and its take-charge personality.

the breed, for in a few short years much of the best breeding stock had been sold abroad, causing a drain on genetic resources and consequently putting the future of the breed in danger.

THE GRANDE MADAME

Madame Harper Trois-Fontaines's de Fontenay Kennel was undisputedly the fountainhead of the breed in Britain, providing stock from which many Pyrenean enthusiasts were able to build their kennels, both at home and abroad. This remarkable lady died in 1972, in her ninety-eighth year.

The first Great Pyrenees known in Ireland arrived in Dublin in 1898, having traveled over from France.

EUROPE IN THE EARLY TWENTIETH CENTURY

It was in 1907 that the Pastoure Club was formed in Hautes Pyrénées, France, with the aim of perpetuating interest in the breed. This led to the first breed standard's being published. Two years later, in 1909, Lady Sybil Grant, daughter of Lord Roseberry, brought Great Pyreneess to England, these for the purpose of breeding. In the early 1920s, Sir

One of the lesser known flock guards, the Tatra Mountain Dog, known as the Owczarek Podhalanski in Poland, is related to the mountain guards of Rumania and Hungary. It is a large, confident breed used to protect flocks as well as estates.

Cato Worsfold also attempted to establish the breed in Britain, but, like Lady Sybil Grant, without significant success.

Unfortunately, during the 1920s the Great Pyrenees declined in both numbers and quality in France, but M. Senac Lagrange and a handful of other dedicated breeders worked hard to revive the breed. Together they formed the Reunion des Amateurs de Chiens Pyrénéens, and this club drew up the breed standard in the mid-1920s. The club still exists today, and its breed standard has been the foundation stone for all Great Pyrenees standards of the modern era.

PURE-BRED PURPOSE

Given the vast range of the world's 400 or so pure breeds of dog, it's fair to say that domestic dogs are the most versatile animal in the kingdom. From the tiny 1-pound lap dog to the 200-pound guard dog, dogs have adapted to every need and whim of their human masters. Humans have selectively bred dogs to alter physical attributes like size, ability, color, leg length, mass and skull diameter in order to suit our own needs and fancies. Dogs serve humans not only as companions and guardians but also as hunters, exterminators, shepherds, rescuers, messengers, warriors, babysitters and more!

In England, it was not until the early 1930s that Mme. Jeanne Harper Trois-Fontaines began her de Fontenay Kennel, which from 1938 was near Amersham in Buckinghamshire. She had first been impressed by the Great Pyreneess she had seen at the Manoir de Careil when vacationing in France with her husband. He suggested that she order a couple, which she did, no doubt willingly, but these did not arrive in Britain until 1933. Unfortunately, they were not allowed to be quarantined together, and they are

> **HELPING THE ST. BERNARD**
> Because the number of St. Bernards had been seriously depleted due to avalanches and distemper at the hospice in Switzerland, in 1870 the blood of Great Pyrenees, and that of other large breeds, was used to help the St. Bernard breed back to recovery.

said both to have died of loneliness before the age of six months. The following year, Madame successfully brought in a ten-

The Kuvasz from Hungary is not as large as its cousin, the Komondor, and enjoys growing popularity in the UK and America.

expense. She also did valuable publicity work on behalf of the breed, not only through dog shows but also with appearances on stage, screen and television. From her kennel, Great Pyrenees were to be exported world-wide.

It appears that it was the late Baron Rothschild who first suggested starting a breed club, this at a tea party at his home in Tring. Seemingly, the very next morning, Mme. Harper Trois-Fontaines went to The Kennel Club to obtain registration papers, and opened a bank account for the club. In 1936 the Pyrenean Mountain Dog Club of Great Britain was registered with The English Kennel Club (although it was to be almost a decade before the club was officially recognized), and, in October of that year, the first breed classes were judged by France's M. Senac Legrange at Crystal Palace.

Take note of this gentle giant. At a dog show in Paris (circa 1930), a Great Pyrenees became a press spectacular. This photo appeared in numerous publications of the day. month-old puppy from the Loire, and she thought very highly of this dog, Kop de Careil. Six months later, the bitch Iannette de Boisy joined him, forming the foundation stock of the renowned de Fontenay kennel.

Madame Harper Trois-Fontaines aimed to import only the most typical bloodlines from France, and in this she spared no

BREED NAMES AND NICKNAMES

Known in Britain and some European countries as the Pyrenean Mountain Dog, the breed has various names around the world. In the US, the breed is known as the Great Pyrenees and, in France, is called Le Chien de Montagne des Pyrénées or Le Chien des Pyrénées. Over 200 years ago, it was also known as the "King of Sheepdogs" and the "White-furred Lord."

FROM WORLD WAR II ONWARD

Throughout out the years of World War II, Mme. Harper Trois-Fontaines continued in her efforts to get the new breed club recognized by The Kennel Club, and over a period of four years managed to register 150 Pyreneans. Membership increased after the war and, in 1945, The Kennel Club gave the club official recognition, allowing Challenge Certificates to be awarded, the "tickets" that are required for British championships. It was headed by the same staunch lady supporter of the breed who was at that point its President, Secretary and Treasurer, though this had not been the case in its formative years. In May 1946, the breed's very first Championship Show was held at Buckingham Gate in London.

Later, due to the controversy surrounding one person's holding three such posts in the breed club, Madame resigned as Secretary and Treasurer. Subsequently the club ran into difficulties, only to be bailed out financially for the second time by Mme. Harper Trois-Fontaines. In 1969, the first Pyrenean Symposium was held, with the aim of furthering knowledge about every aspect of the breed.

The Pyrenean Mountain Dog Club of Great Britain still exists, and is one of four clubs now in Britain. In 1996, a Diamond Jubilee Banquet was held, together with the first World Congress, which took place at Coventry. This was an opportunity for enthusiasts from all over the world to get together and share their ideas about the breed, and there was a plentiful supply of knowledgeable speakers from as far apart as Scandinavia and Australia.

THE PYRENEAN AS A CARTING DOG

Great Pyrenees were used for pulling small carts until fairly recent times. This was particularly so in Belgium and northern

Mountain Dogs photographed in the Pyrenean Mountains early in the 20th century illustrate the type of working dog that existed about 100 years ago.

France, where they delivered milk, like many other of the carting dogs. Although today the subject of carting causes controversy in some circles, some breed enthusiasts still use their dogs to pull small, light-weight carts as a hobby.

PYRENEANS AS LIVESTOCK GUARDIANS

This breed's original role in the Pyrenean Mountains region was that of livestock guardian, but now in many countries the Great Pyrenees is kept purely as a companion and show dog. However, in some countries the breed is still employed successfully for its original purpose. A livestock guardian dog is neither a hunter nor a shepherd, but it does show a protective attitude toward its stock and will fend off predators upon the animals that it considers as its own property.

In the US, toward the close of the 1970s, there was renewed interest in using the Pyrenean as a livestock guardian dog, as new methods of preventing the loss of stock to predators were needed. Among various breeds considered, the Pyrenean was found to be well suited to the job. It had kept its original instincts, yet still showed good-natured behavior with people, and so made an admirable family companion.

In recent years, Great Pyreneess performed an interesting exercise in Norway, close to the borders of Russia and Finland, where bears were entering a village. A long-standing Norwegian breeder of Pyreneans worked in cooperation with the Norwegian environmental organization, which placed six puppies on three farms. This understandably caused some concern among breeders, who thought the breed would run the risk of obtaining a bad reputation, thereby losing its popularity as a family dog.

Although the dogs used had chased foxes, it was not known whether they would apply the same principles to chasing off bears. The outcome, however, was that the dogs were indeed effective, showing a high fighting spirit around the bears and completing their mission without injury. Despite resistance from the bears, the dogs maintained their interest in their work and could cope with physical contact with the bears without sustaining injury or becoming nervous. Added to this, they took their own responsibility for livestock in their neighborhood; on two occasions of accidental encounters with bears, the dogs showed guarding attitudes towards their owners, scaring off the bears.

One of the farmers was so impressed that he subsequently took on two Great Pyreneess of his own. Soon after, although bears were still found at the northern and southern ends of the village, they did not enter the village center, as they had done in previous years.

THE GREAT PYRENEES IN AMERICA

The first pair of Great Pyrenees was introduced to America in 1824 by General Lafayette, who took two males to J. S. Skinner, author of *The Dog and the Sportsman.* Although there were a few imports following these, the breed in the US was really launched when the Basquaerie Kennel was founded in Massachusetts in 1931. This was the largest kennel of the breed ever established, and stock produced from this source provided many smaller kennels, both in the US and abroad, with dogs.

The early days of the breed in the US were relatively informal, with people happy to cooperate in supporting and promoting the breed. Owners and breeders all worked together in helping to standardize the breed and to improve it.

In 1933 the Great Pyrenees was given official recognition by the American Kennel Club. By April of that year, there was separate classification for the breed at shows. In 1935, the breed standard, which had been based on the French standard of the 1920s, was revised, remaining unchanged for a further 55 years.

EARLY SHOWS

The first time a Great Pyrenees appeared in a dog show in the US was on February 21, 1932 at Boston's Eastern Dog Club Chow. Here Urdos de Soum won the Miscellaneous Class. Then in 1934 Ch. Patou, one of the Basquaerie dogs, took the Working Group at Middlesex County Kennel Club Show.

Specialty shows began in 1935 at the Morris and Essex Show, held on the famous Giralda Farms Estate in Madison, NJ. Urdos de Soum again achieved success at this show, winning the class for dogs of 25 pounds and over. Mitsou de Langladure won the equivalent class for bitches. Members and friends of the Great Pyrenees Club of America, which had been officially recognized by the AKC on September 10, 1935, donated special prizes for the winners.

By January of 1936 there were 41 Great Pyrenees living in the US, 17 of which had been

Slovak Cuvac is the Czech equivalent to the Pyrenean Mountain Dog. It is a large white guardian breed utilized to protect flocks in the Liptok Mountains. Rarely seen outside the Czech Republic, the breed is sometimes called Slovensky Tchouvatch.

imported. There were three litters whelped in 1933, two in 1934 and seven in 1935. Clearly, the breed was on the road to success!

GROWTH OF THE GREAT PYRENEES CLUB OF AMERICA

The first 15 years of the club's existence experienced substantial growth, with plenty of activity and publicity, but there was little growth during the 1950s and 1960s, in part because until the mid-1960s bylaws limited the membership to fifty. However by the 1970s the breed had further increased in popularity so membership continued to rise again and by the 1990s membership was in excess of 700.

An example of a Great Pyrenees that worked for the military is M. Dretzen's Ch. Eng. Porthos, photographed in 1907.

Two Great Pyrenees photographed in the early 1930s. The dog on the left was well known in its day, Eng. Ch. Thora.

There are many regional clubs who all have members with the breed's best interest at heart. They, too, organize all manner of events in their local areas, and provide information and assistance to owners of the breed.

Today in the US, the Great Pyrenees is found in the show ring but is also much loved as a companion in the home; the breed is also used on farms and ranches as a livestock guardian.

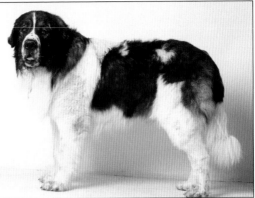

A breed of increasing importance in Spain is the Mastin del Pireneo, known in English-speaking countries as the Pyrenean Mastiff. Unlike most of the other large flock guards, the Mastin del Pireneo can be seen in white with grey, black, brindle or orange. The breed is long-coated, unlike its cousin the Mastin Español.

PYRENEANS IN NEW ZEALAND
Pyreneans from England's de Fontenay Kennel went to New Zealand in the late 1940s. Early in the next decade, two Pyreneans from the Pondtail Kennel were imported and kept at Auckland Zoo, the latter producing a small litter. However, it was not until 1956 that the breeding of Great Pyrenees began in earnest in New Zealand. There were imports from Britain in the 1950s and 1960s, but there are some sad stories among them, due primarily to the long journey involved and the time spent in quarantine.

There was a poor survival rate in litters whelped, and the selection of stock from which to breed was limited, so numbers did not increase greatly. Despite this, some Pyreneans went to Australia at this time. In New Zealand the breed became firmly established in the 1970s and 1980s, with imports from England and also from Australia. The first NZ Champion was Cherryglen Elizabeth, an import from Britain, and it was she who produced the first two NZ-bred champions.

Over recent years, breeders have continued to import stock from prominent kennels in Britain, the US and Australia, but the number of kennels in New Zealand can be counted on two hands. Nonetheless, Great Pyrenees always attract the crowds when they are seen in public, and apart from winning at Group level at dog shows, they can also be seen collecting for charity. Because New Zealand has no natural predators, there is little use for dogs as livestock guardians in the country— although Pyreneans always seem ready to take over the supervision of a few sheep in a paddock if the opportunity arises.

CHARACTERISTICS OF THE
GREAT PYRENEES

WHY THE GREAT PYRENEES?
The Great Pyrenees is undoubtedly a magnificent animal, one that has a deep devotion to its family and home, but also an inborn instinct to guard and protect. When considering whether or not this is the dog for them, would-be owners should also take into account the great size of this breed. As a puppy, a Great is a lovable little ball of fluff, but it will quickly grow into a very large dog. Thus it will need environmental surroundings to suit, and an owner must be physically capable of handing such a powerful dog. The owner must be able to provide the dog with a large, securely fenced area for sufficient exercise.

Choice of a breed with a profuse light-colored coat is also something to be taken into account, for a Great Pyrenees with a dirty ungroomed coat looks very different from the beautifully presented animal with which one

Are you ready to enter into the world of this majestic guardian breed? "They don't call me the *Great* Pyrenees for nothing!"

may be familiar from seeing in the show ring.

PERSONALITY
This is an intelligent breed that is trustworthy and affectionate. Although gentle and tractable, Great Pyrenees will be protective of those they consider their "property," as well as protective of their territory. As watchdogs, they certainly command respect, but they also make wonderful pets and are very devoted to their families and homes, needing regular love and attention.

Facing page: The Great Pyrenees's height is usually measured at *its* shoulders—not yours! This is a mountain of a dog that requires a committed, capable owner to love.

This is a natural guardian, capable of and willing to protect flocks and shepherds, originally from wolves and bears. It should always be borne in mind that Pyreneans were bred to be left alone in the mountain valleys with sheep and that their guarding ability is instinctive, not a result of training. This is a dog that was bred to work alone, without taking commands from people; as such, their personality is rather different from that of most breeds. They can sometimes be rather willful and, although there are undoubtedly a few Great Pyrenees who take part in obedience, in general they are not easily trained to obedience. Many Pyreneans are very

The Great Pyrenees was bred to work alone, protecting the flocks from wolves and bears. They thrive on outdoor work and responsibility as well as companionship and proper care.

independent and do not necessarily give importance to the same things as humans might!

The breed standard says that the breed should be "confident, gentle and affectionate," pointing out that "any sign of excessive shyness, nervousness or aggression to humans is unacceptable." This is especially important in such a large breed, for a Great Pyrenees with untypical instability of temperament would be extremely difficult to control.

Although boisterous up to the age of about two, once a Great Pyrenees has reached full maturity it will be placid by nature and calm around the home. It likes its life to be consistent and predictable, and will enjoy quiet periods in which it may rest comfortably and sleep undisturbed.

In common with other livestock-guarding breeds, Great

A NATURAL GUARD

This is a guarding breed, and consequently it is only natural that Pyreneans cannot be expected to welcome unwanted visitors! Although not "attack" dogs, their very size and demeanor can be intimidating. However, they will be ready to accept anyone who has been invited to the home. It is therefore important for owners to treat this breed's natural guarding instinct in a responsible manner.

Pyrenees will bark, and some owners feel that they do so especially at night. This is one of several reasons for this breed's being best suited to country living, or certainly to a home with understanding neighbors.

PHYSICAL CHARACTERISTICS

This is a breed of great size, substance and power. It looks immensely strong and is well balanced, while the attractive coat and splendid head impart a degree of elegance.

Size

The breed standard stipulates a minimum height of 27 inches at shoulder for dogs and 25 inches for bitches, and many are considerably taller than this. This is perfectly in order, provided that type and character are retained.

Weight needs to be in proportion to height, for the Great

WEIGHING A LARGE BREED

A Great Pyrenees is a big breed to weigh, so one cannot use the more usual method of weighing yourself while holding the dog and then subtracting your own weight to obtain the difference. A solution is to use two sets of scales. Stand the dog's front legs on one scale and the hind legs on the other, and then add up the two weights. This shouldn't be too difficult, if your Pyrenean will stand still!

EXERCISE AND AFFECTION
Great Pyrenees need substantial outside exercise areas, but they thrive on love and affection and need to play an important part in the home lives of their owners. Pyreneans left alone, without companionship, become lonely and bored, and bored dogs can become destructive ones.

Pyrenees is a powerful animal with great strength. This means, however, that dogs should not carry excess fat. The breed standard indicates that the minimal-height male (27 inches) should weigh about 100 pounds, and the minimal-height female (25 inches) should weigh 85 pounds.

Even though the Great Pyrenees is a good house dog and is very happy around the home, because of the breed's great size it is imperative that it also has access to a substantial outside area for exercise. Because it is the breed's instinct to patrol its territory, the area to which it is confined should be well fenced to give the dog a sense of his borders.

HEAD, EYES AND EARS
The head of the Great Pyrenees is strong, but in no way coarse, and should not be too heavy in relation to the dog's size. The top of the head has a definite curve, giving a domed effect. The American Kennel Club breed standard gives a clear description of the head features and relevant proportions.

The almond-shaped eyes are a beautiful dark amber-brown in color. The eyelids should not droop, but should be close-fitting and bordered with black, just as the nose pigment is black. The fairly small ears are triangular in shape, with rounded tips. Although they normally lie flat against the head, they may be slightly raised when the dog is alert.

TAIL
The Great Pyrenees's tail is thickly coated with rather long hair, forming a most attractive plume. When in repose, the tail is carried low, the tip turning slightly to one side; the tail rises and curls high above the back in a circle when the dog is fully interested and alert.

MOVEMENT

Great Pyrenees generally move in an unhurried fashion, steady and smooth, but are well capable of producing bursts of speed when they deem it necessary. When moving slowly, this breed has a tendency to pace, which means that the left fore- and hind legs advance in unison, followed by the right fore- and hind legs, and so on.

COAT AND COLOR

The Great Pyrenees's stunning coat is surely one of many attractive features of this majestic breed. There is a profuse undercoat of fine hairs, while the outer coat is of coarser texture. The outer coat is thick, and though it may be straight or slightly wavy, it should never be curly or fuzzy. Around the neck and shoulders, the coat forms a mane, which is usually less developed in bitches, and the coat is longer toward the tail. The forelegs are fringed, and the long, woolly hair behind the thighs gives the effect of pantaloons. Bitches tend to be more smooth coated than males.

This breed is predominantly white in color, but there may be patches of badger, gray, reddish brown or tan. If present, color patches may be on the head, ears or base of tail, and a few are permissible on the body. Black patches that go right down to the root of the hair are highly undesirable.

HEAVY AND HEAVIER

We all know that Great Pyrenees are large, heavy dogs, but if you try to coax a Pyrenees into something he doesn't want to do, he only seems to get heavier! It has been said that on the first day at a training class, a Great Pyrenees weighs as much as a small elephant. When trying to teach the down/stay in an obedience class, the dog's weight is that of a Sumo wrestler. And if one tries to administer a pill or cut toenails, the Pyrenees can resemble a moray eel!

Maintaining a good healthy clean coat on a Great Pyrenees is important, so a thorough brushing and combing session is needed about three times each week. Pyreneans do shed their coats, so owners must be prepared to find lots of white hairs around the home and on their clothes! In general, dogs drop their coats just once each year, and bitches twice, usually following their seasons.

Teeth still in place but slightly worn down in this bitch over ten years old.

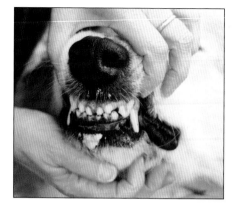

BOREDOM SPELLS TROUBLE

A Great Pyrenees that is left alone in the home will almost certainly become bored, and a large bored dog can become a highly destructive one! A bored Pyrenees may decide to chew, and he will probably not take into account which are and which are not your favorite possessions, so be forewarned.

MOUTH AND TEETH

Generally, the Great Pyrenees has a scissors bite, in which the upper teeth closely overlap the lower ones; this is the typical mouth formation for most canines. However, a level bite, in which the teeth meet edge to edge, is also tolerated in this breed. It is important that the teeth are strong, healthy and even (although the two central lower incisors may be set a little deeper than the others), and dentition should be complete. Lips should be tight-fitting, and the roof of the mouth and the lips are either black or heavily marked with black. It is interesting to note that, because of the tight-fitting lip formation, the Great Pyrenees does not drool or salivate as much as many of the other giant breeds.

FEATURES OF THE FEET

A rather unusual feature of this breed is that Great Pyrenees have strong double dewclaws on their hind legs. This is something that is required by the breed standard, so is a necessity for exhibition purposes. They should be two completely separate claws, which can be clearly distinguished as two separate toes. It is important that dewclaws be trimmed regularly, as they do not wear down naturally. Although the reason for the breed's having double dewclaws is not certain, it is believed that they may have had a "snow-shoe" effect. Pyreneans usually have single dewclaws on the front feet, and occasionally these, too, are double. The feet themselves are short and compact, with slightly arched toes and strong nails.

HEALTH CONSIDERATIONS

All breeds encounter health problems of one sort or another, but the Great Pyrenees is basically a very healthy breed with few major problems. As time moves on, and as genetic research progresses, clubs dedicated to the breed have begun to conduct health surveys. It is

THE GENTLE GIANT
Despite its imposing size, the Great Pyrenees is of a gentle nature, and is especially good with children. Its size in comparison with that of a small child should, however, be borne in mind when introductions are made, and one should always be aware that until the age of about two, Pyrenees can be rather boisterous.

therefore to be expected that more and more problems will come to light, and this can only be for the future benefit of the breed.

To be forewarned is to be forearmed, so the following section of this chapter is not intended to put fear into those who are considering becoming owners of Great Pyrenees. Instead I hope it will help to enlighten them so that any health problems encountered can be dealt with as early as possible and in the most appropriate manner.

The strong double dewclaws on the hind legs are, in fact, two additional toes. They should be present.

Do You Know about Hip Dysplasia?

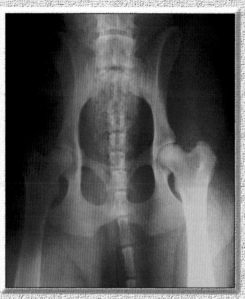

X-ray of a dog with "Good" hips.

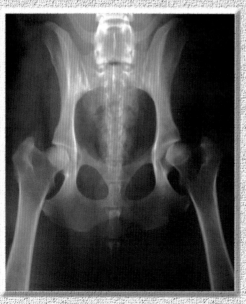

X-ray of a dog with "Moderate" dysplastic hips.

Hip dysplasia is a fairly common condition found in pure-bred dogs. When a dog has hip dysplasia, his hind leg has an incorrectly formed hip joint. By constant use of the hip joint, it becomes more and more loose, wears abnormally and may become arthritic.

Hip dysplasia can only be confirmed with an x-ray, but certain symptoms may indicate a problem. Your dog may have a hip dysplasia problem if he walks in a peculiar manner, hops instead of smoothly runs, uses his hind legs in unison (to keep the pressure off the weak joint), has trouble getting up from a prone position or always sits with both legs together on one side of his body.

As the dog matures, he may adapt well to life with a bad hip, but in a few years the arthritis develops, and many dogs with hip dysplasia become crippled.

Hip dysplasia is considered an inherited disease and only can be diagnosed definitively by x-ray when the dog is two years old, although symptoms often appear earlier. Some experts claim that a special diet might help your puppy outgrow the bad hip, but the usual treatments are surgical. The removal of the pectineus muscle, the removal of the round part of the femur, reconstructing the pelvis and replacing the hip with an artificial one are all surgical interventions that are expensive, but they are usually very successful. Follow the advice of your veterinarian.

HIP DYSPLASIA

HD, as it is commonly known, is a problem involving the malformation of the ball-and-socket joint at the hip, a developmental condition caused by the interaction of many genes. This results in looseness of the hip joints and, although not always painful, it can cause lameness and can impair typical movement.

Hip dysplasia is not a major problem within the breed, but a few cases do occur, and some breeders have their dogs' hips evalutated. Both hips are tested and scored individually; the lower the score, the less the degree of dysplasia.

Clearly, it is sensible that serious thought be given to using dogs with high scores in breeding programs, and elimination from a breeding program may have to be considered. It is worth bearing in mind that a Great Pyrenees is a particularly large breed to x-ray, so some breeders feel it wise to discuss with their vets exactly how this is to be done so that as true a reading as possible can be obtained.

Although a dog's environment does not actually cause hip dysplasia, it may have some bearing on how unstable the hip joint eventually becomes. Osteoarthritis can eventually develop as a result of the instability.

DELTA SOCIETY

The human-animal bond propels the work of the Delta Society, striving to improve the lives of people and animals. The Pet Partners Program proves that the lives of people and dogs are inextricably linked. The Pet Partners Program, a national registry, trains and screens volunteers for pet therapy in hospices, nursing homes, schools and rehabilitation centers. Dog-and-handler teams of Pet Partners volunteer in all 50 states, with nearly 7,000 teams making visits annually. About 900,000 patients, residents and students receive assistance each year. If you and your dog are interested in becoming Pet Partners, contact the Delta Society online at www.deltasociety.org.

SLEEPING ARRANGEMENTS

A warm, dry place to sleep is essential for a Great Pyrenees. Most seem to prefer to sleep on a hard surface rather than on a carpet, but a Great Pyrenees will usually not take exception to his owner's comfortable bed! This can be somewhat of an inconvenience, especially if your Great Pyrenees snores, which some do.

BONE GROWTH

As this is a very large breed, with rapid bone growth, young puppies should not have much lead work on hard pavements; this can lead to problems later in life. Of course they may have short walks, for they will need to become accustomed to their leads, but exercise of this kind must be restricted up to the age of about one year. Most breeders, however, allow their youngsters as much free exercise as they want, although the pups should not be permitted to jump down from high levels.

SKIN PROBLEMS AND ALLERGIES

Some Great Pyrenees seem rather susceptible to skin problems and allergies, although this, of course, is by no means unique to this breed. The reasons behind these problems can be many.

Damp coats can play an important part here, for skin trouble can result if coats are not dried thoroughly. It is also important to groom out any old coat, especially during a molt, for this can also give rise to skin problems.

A common allergy is that to flea saliva and flea bites, making it doubly important that your dog is not plagued by these unwanted parasites. Obviously dogs that have access to farmland may pick up the occasional tick, so owners must be on the lookout for these unwanted creatures too!

Another type of skin irritation, known as a "hot spot," often contains a small brown dry spot in its center. It is important that owners do not allow infection to set up as a result.

EYE PROBLEMS

The most frequent eye problem found in the Great Pyrenees is distichiasis, in which extra hairs grow along the edge of the eyelid and rub along the surface of the cornea. Generally a young dog grows out of this condition with maturity; as the face "fills out," the offending eyelashes are pulled

HEART-HEALTHY

In this modern age of ever-improving cardio-care, no doctor or scientist can dispute the advantages of owning a dog to lower a person's risk of heart disease. Studies have proven that petting a dog, walking a dog and grooming a dog all show positive results toward lowering a person's blood pressure. The simple routine of exercising your dog—going outside with the dog and walking, jogging or playing catch—is heart-healthy in and of itself. If you are normally less active than your physician thinks you should be, adopting a dog may be a smart option to improve your own quality of life as well as that of another creature.

been left wet following exercise outdoors. It is therefore absolutely essential to dry the coat thoroughly and that it not be allowed to remain damp.

As in other breeds, occasionally bone cancers and other cancers are diagnosed in elderly dogs. Thankfully, gastric torsion (bloat) seems not to be a problem, and heart problems do not arise any more frequently than usual.

The Great Pyrenees's eyes should be checked regularly by the veterinarian, and any dogs intended for breeding should be screened before planning a mating.

away from the eye, causing no further problem. Obviously veterinary attention should be sought should the matter not rectify itself as a youngster grows older.

RARELY ENCOUNTERED PROBLEMS
A very few Great Pyrenees have been known to suffer from patellar luxation, a substandard formation of the knee joint. In mild cases, there may be no evident sign of the problem; more severe cases can be both painful and disabling, and arthritis can develop in the long term.

Another cause of arthritis, which can sometimes be found in older dogs, is when the coat has

GREAT PYRENEES

The breed standard is the guideline for all breeders, judges and exhibitors. The dog that most closely conforms to the standard, in the judge's opinion, is the dog that will win in the show ring.

When discussing the history of the breed, you will recall that attention was attracted by van Bylandt's description of the Great Pyrenees in his encyclopedia *Les Races de Chiens*. This book was a much enlarged "second" edition, published in 1897, with a subse-quent edition in 1904. Although the wording used then was much more scant, much of the description, in essence, has the same meaning. However, a few comments will surely raise the odd eyebrow, such as that the muzzle was "rather snipey." There was also quite a difference in color, for the section on color read, "All white. (Sometimes small orange patches on the ears.)" Height then ranged from 26 to 30 inches, and weight was given as 135 to 155 lbs.

All breed standards are designed effectively to paint a picture in words, though each reader will almost certainly have a slightly different way of interpreting these words. After all, when all is said and done, were every-one to interpret a breed's standard in exactly the same way, there would only be one consistent winner within the breed at any given time!

In any event, to fully compre-hend the intricacies of a breed, reading words alone is never enough. In addition, it is essential for devotees to watch other Great Pyrenees being judged at shows and, if possible, to attend semi-nars at which the breed is

discussed. This enables owners to absorb as much as possible about their chosen breed of dog. "Hands on" experience, providing an opportunity to assess the structure of dogs, is always valuable, especially for those who hope ultimately to judge the breed.

A breed standard undoubtedly helps breeders to produce stock that comes as close as possible to the recognized standard, and helps judges to know exactly what they are looking for. This enables a judge to make a carefully considered decision when selecting the most typical Great Pyrenees present to head his line of winners.

However familiar one is with the breed, it is always worth refreshing one's memory by re-reading the standard, for it is sometimes all too easy to overlook, or perhaps conveniently forget, certain features.

THE AMERICAN KENNEL CLUB STANDARD FOR THE GREAT PYRENEES

GENERAL APPEARANCE

The Great Pyrenees dog conveys the distinct impression of elegance and unsurpassed beauty combined with great overall size and majesty. He has a white or principally white coat that may contain markings of badger, gray, or varying shades of tan. He possesses a keen intelligence and

a kindly, while regal, expression. Exhibiting a unique elegance of bearing and movement, his soundness and coordination show unmistakably the purpose for which he has been bred, the strenuous work of guarding the flocks in all kinds of weather on the steep mountain slopes of the Pyrenees.

SIZE, PROPORTION, SUBSTANCE

Size: The height at the withers ranges from 27 inches to 32 inches for dogs and from 25 inches to 29 inches for bitches. A 27 inch dog weighs about 100 pounds and a 25 inch bitch weighs about 85 pounds. Weight is in proportion to the overall size and structure. *Proportion:* The Great Pyrenees is a balanced dog with the height measured at the withers being somewhat less than the length of the body measured from the point of the shoulder to the rearmost projection of the

The gait of the Great Pyrenees is as vital to the breed as its physical conformation and temperament. The breed should move with an unhurried steady and smooth gait.

Great Pyrenees head study, showing desirable type, proportion and balance.

upper thigh (buttocks). These proportions create a somewhat rectangular dog, slightly longer than it is tall. Front and rear angulation are balanced. *Substance:* The Great Pyrenees is a dog of medium substance whose coat deceives those who do not feel the bone and muscle. Commensurate with his size and impression of elegance there is sufficient bone and muscle to provide a balance with the frame. *Faults:* Size—Dogs and bitches under minimum size or over maximum size. Substance—Dogs too heavily boned or too lightly boned to be in balance with their frame.

HEAD

Correct head and expression are essential to the breed. The head is not heavy in proportion to the size of the dog. It is wedge shaped with a slightly rounded crown. *Expression:* The expression is elegant, intelligent and contemplative. *Eyes:* Medium sized, almond shaped, set slightly obliquely, rich dark brown. Eyelids are close fitting with black rims. *Ears:* Small to medium in size, V-shaped with rounded tips, set on at eye level, normally carried low, flat, and close to the head. There is a characteristic meeting of the hair of the upper and lower face which forms a line from the outer corner of the eye to the base of the ear. *Skull and Muzzle:* The muzzle is approximately equal in length to the back skull. The width and length of the skull are approximately equal. The muzzle blends smoothly with the skull. The cheeks are flat. There is sufficient fill under the eyes. A slight furrow exists between the eyes. There is no apparent stop. The boney eyebrow ridges are only slightly developed. Lips are tight fitting with the upper lip just covering the lower lip. There is a strong lower jaw. The nose and lips are black. *Teeth:* A scissor bite is preferred,

Body study, illustrating correct balance, substance and type.

HEAD AND BODY FAULTS IN PROFILE

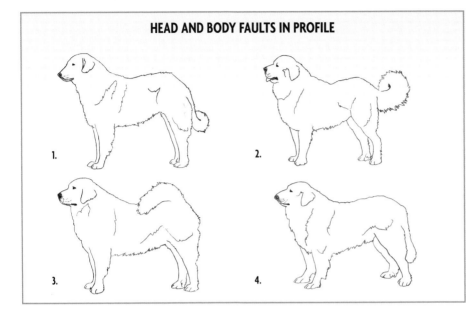

1.

2.

3.

4.

1. Poor facial pigment, lacking stop, snipey, ears set too high; upright shoulders, too high on leg, flat feet, dip behind withers, high in rear, lacking rear angulation, kinked tail.

2. Heavy dewlap, excessively domed topskull; upright shoulders, toes out in front, very weak topline, cow-hocked behind, excessive curl at end of tail.

3. Upright, loaded shoulders, toes out in front, weak straight rear, improper tail carriage.

4. Roman nose; short neck, long back, soft topline, high in rear, weak pasterns, flat feet, upright shoulders, weak rear, cow-hocked.

but a level bite is acceptable. It is not unusual to see dropped (receding) lower central incisor teeth. *Faults:* Too heavy head (St. Bernard or Newfoundland-like). Too narrow or small skull. Foxy appearance. Presence of an apparent stop. Missing pigmentation on nose, eye rims, or lips. Eyelids round, triangular, loose or small. Overshot, undershot, wry mouth.

NECK, TOPLINE, BODY

Neck: Strongly muscled and of medium length, with minimal dewlap. *Topline:* The backline is level. *Body:* The chest is moderately broad. The rib cage is well sprung, oval in shape, and of sufficient depth to reach the elbows. Back and loin are broad and strongly coupled with some tuck-up. The croup is gently sloping with the tail set on just below the level of the back. *Tail:* The tailbones are of sufficient length to reach the hock. The tail is well plumed, carried low in repose and may be carried over the back, "making the wheel," when aroused. When present, a "shepherd's crook" at the end of the tail accentuates the plume. When gaiting, the tail may be carried either over the back or low. Both carriages are equally correct. *Fault:* Barrel ribs.

FOREQUARTERS

Shoulders: The shoulders are well laid back, well muscled, and lie

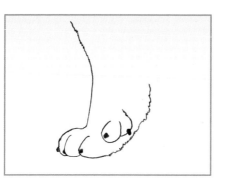

close to the body. The upper arm meets the shoulder blade at approximately a right angle. The upper arm angles backward from the point of the shoulder to the elbow and is never perpendicular to the ground. The length of the shoulder blade and the upper arm is approximately equal. The height from the ground to the elbow appears approximately equal to the height from the elbow to the withers. *Forelegs:* The legs are of sufficient bone and muscle to provide a balance with the frame. The elbows are close to the body and point directly to the rear when standing and gaiting. The forelegs, when viewed from the side, are located directly under the withers and are straight and vertical to the ground. The elbows, when viewed from the front, are set in a straight line from the point of shoulder to the wrist. Front pasterns are strong and flexible. Each foreleg carries a single dewclaw. *Front Feet:* Rounded, close-cupped, well padded, toes well arched.

HINDQUARTERS

The angulation of the hindquarters is similar in degree to that of the forequarters. *Thighs:* Strongly muscular upper thighs extend from the pelvis at right angles. The upper thigh is the same length as the lower thigh, creating moderate stifle joint angulation when viewed in profile. The rear pastern (metatarsus) is of medium length and perpendicular to the ground as the dog stands naturally. This produces a moderate degree of angulation in the hock joint, when viewed from the side. The hindquarters from the hip to the rear pastern are straight and parallel, as viewed from the rear. The rear legs are of sufficient bone and muscle to provide a balance with the frame. Double dewclaws are located on each rear leg. *Rear Feet:* The rear feet have a structural tendency to toe out slightly. This breed characteristic is not to be confused with cow-hocks. The rear feet, like the forefeet, are rounded, close-cupped, well padded with toes well arched. *Fault:* Absence of double dewclaws on each rear leg.

COAT

The weather resistant double coat consists of a long, flat, thick, outer coat of coarse hair, straight or slightly undulating, and lying over a dense, fine, woolly undercoat. The coat is more profuse about the neck and shoulders where it forms a ruff or mane which is more pronounced in males. Longer hair on the tail forms a plume. There is feathering along the back of the front legs and along the back of the thighs, giving a "pantaloon" effect. The hair on the face and ears is shorter and of finer texture. Correctness of coat is more important than abundance of coat. *Faults:* Curly coat. Stand-off coat (Samoyed type).

COLOR

White or white with markings of gray, badger, reddish brown, or varying shades of tan. Markings of varying size may appear on the ears, head (including a full face mask), tail, and as a few body spots. The undercoat may be white or shaded. All of the above described colorings and locations are characteristic of the breed and equally correct. *Fault:* Outer coat markings covering more than one third of the body.

GAIT

The Great Pyrenees moves smoothly and elegantly, true and straight ahead, exhibiting both power and agility. The stride is well balanced with good reach and strong drive. The legs tend to move toward the center line as speed increases. Ease and efficiency of movement are more important than speed.

TEMPERAMENT

Character and temperament are of utmost importance. In nature, the Great Pyrenees is confident, gentle, and affectionate. While territorial and protective of his flock or family when necessary, his general demeanor is one of

quiet composure, both patient and tolerant. He is strong willed, independent and somewhat reserved, yet attentive, fearless and loyal to his charges both human and animal.

Although the Great Pyrenees may appear reserved in the show ring, any sign of excessive shyness, nervousness, or aggression to humans is unacceptable and must be considered an extremely serious fault.

Approved June 12, 1990
Effective August 1, 1990

The Great Pyrenees possesses a profuse undercoat of fine hairs and a coarser outer coat, colored solid white, with patches of yellow, wolf-gray and/or badger on the head, ears and base of tail.

GREAT PYRENEES

HOW TO SELECT A PUPPY

Before reaching the decision that you will definitely look for a Great Pyrenees puppy, it is essential that you are clear in your mind that this is absolutely the most suitable breed for you and your family. A puppy grows rapidly, and the breed's great size will undoubtedly be one of the first things to take into account, as your home environment and surroundings must be suitable. A Great Pyrenees usually reaches full height by about ten months, but continues to develop bodily until the age of two and a half years.

Also take into account that the white coat will shed, especially when moulting, so it is inevitable that you will find long white hairs around your home and on your clothes.

The temperament is quietly confident and usually very stable, but one should not lose sight of the fact that the Great Pyrenees also has a natural guarding instinct. It is essential therefore that any puppy showing signs of nervousness or unprovoked aggression be avoided. Such temperament is very rare in the

breed, and is never to be encouraged.

Once you are certain that this is the breed for you, you must also ask yourself why you want a Great Pyrenees; do you want one purely as a pet or as a show dog? This should be made clear to the breeder when you make your initial inquiries. If you are seeking a potential show dog, you will need to take the breeder's advice as to which available puppy shows the most promise for the show ring. If looking for a pet, you should discuss your family situation with the breeder and take his advice as to which puppy is likely to suit best. The average litter for the Great Pyrenees is six puppies, but they

At nine weeks of age, these dynamic mountain pups are ready to begin their lives with their new families.

Facing page: Locating a qualified proven breeder is the key to finding the Pyrenees puppy of your dreams. These two six-week-old angels are destined to make two owners' dreams come true. Breeder, Beryl Lord (Laudley).

can have litters as large as 12 or even more; thus, selection will be considerable once you've located a breeder and litter.

When you have your first opportunity to visit the most potentially suitable litter, watch the puppies interact together. You will find that different puppies have different personalities, and some will be more boisterous and extroverted than others. Although

TEMPERAMENT ABOVE ALL ELSE

Regardless of breed, a puppy's disposition is perhaps his most important quality. It is, after all, what makes a puppy lovable and "livable." If the puppy's parents or grandparents are known to be snappy or aggressive, the puppy is likely to inherit those tendencies. That can lead to serious problems, such as the dog's becoming a biter, which can lead to eventual abandonment.

you will need to use your own judgment as to which one is most likely to fit in with your lifestyle, if the breeder you have selected is a good one, you will also be guided by his or her judgment and knowledge of the dogs.

You should have done plenty of background research on the breed, and preferably have visited a few all-breed or specialty shows. Shows give you an opportunity to see the breed in some numbers, plus the chance to observe the dogs with their breeders and owners.

Remember that the dog you select should remain with you for the duration of its life, which will hopefully be ten or more years, so making the right decision from the outset is of utmost importance. No dog should be moved from one home to another simply because its owners were thoughtless enough not to have done sufficient "homework" before selecting the breed. It is always important to remember that, when you are looking for a puppy, a good breeder will be assessing you as a prospective new owner just as carefully as you are selecting the breeder.

Puppies almost invariably look enchanting, but you must select one from a caring breeder who has given the puppies all the attention they deserve and has looked after them well. The puppy you select should look well fed, but not pot-bellied, as this might indicate worms. Eyes should look bright and clear, without discharge. The nose should be moist, which is an indication of good health, but should never be runny. It goes without saying that there should certainly be no evidence of loose bowels or of parasites. The puppy you choose should also have a healthy-looking coat, an important indication of good health internally. Always check the bite of your selected puppy to be sure that it is neither overshot nor undershot. This may not be too noticeable on a young puppy, but will become more evident as the puppy gets older.

SOME DAM ATTITUDE

When selecting a puppy, be certain to meet the dam of the litter. The temperament of the dam is often predictive of the temperament of her puppies. However, dams occasionally are very protective of their young, some to the point of being testy or aggressive with visitors, whom they may view as a danger to their babies. Such attitudes are more common when the pups are very young and still nursing and should not be mistaken for actual aggressive temperament. If possible, visit the dam away from her pups to make friends with her and gain a better understanding of her true personality.

The author Juliette Cunliffe, making the acquaintance of a handsome nine-week-old puppy.

Sex differences in the breed may also affect your choice of a puppy. Do you want a male or a female? In the Great Pyrenees, males are generally larger and carry more coat than females, especially around the mane. Males are not usually tolerant of each other unless they have been raised together, so males often need to be kept separately.

Something else to consider is whether or not to take out veterinary insurance. Vets' bills can mount up, and you must always be certain that sufficient funds are available to give your dog any veterinary attention that may be needed. Keep in mind, though, that routine vaccinations will not be covered.

SELECTING A BREEDER
If you are convinced that the Great Pyrenees is the ideal dog for you, it's time to learn about where to find a puppy and what to look for. Locating a litter of Great Pyrenees should not present a problem for the new owner. You should inquire about breeders in your area who enjoy a good reputation in the breed. You are looking for an established breeder with outstanding dog ethics and a strong commitment to the breed. New owners should have as many questions as they have doubts. An established breeder is indeed the one to answer your four million questions and make you comfortable with your choice of the Great Pyrenees. An established breeder will sell you a puppy at a fair price if, and only if, the breeder determines that you are a suitable worthy owner of his dogs. An established breeder can be relied upon for advice, no matter what time of day or night. A reputable breeder will accept a puppy back, without questions, should you decide that this is not the right dog for you.

When choosing a breeder, reputation is much more important than convenience of

PEDIGREE VS. REGISTRATION CERTIFICATE
Too often new owners are confused between these two important documents. Your puppy's pedigree, essentially a family tree, is a written record of a dog's genealogy of three generations or more. The pedigree will show you the names as well as performance titles of all dogs in your pup's background. Your breeder must provide you with a registration application, with his part properly filled out. You must complete the application and send it to the AKC with the proper fee. Every puppy must come from a litter that has been AKC-registered by the breeder, born in the US and from a sire and dam that are also registered with the AKC.

The seller must provide you with complete records to identify the puppy. The AKC requires that the seller provide the buyer with the following: breed; sex, color and markings; date of birth; litter number (when available); names and registration numbers of the parents; breeder's name; and date sold or delivered.

location. Do not be overly impressed by breeders who run brag advertisements in the presses about their stupendous champions. The real quality breeders are quiet and unassuming. Take advantage of resources available at the shows and from the breed club and AKC.

Choosing a breeder is an important first step in dog ownership. Fortunately, the majority of Great Pyrenees breeders are devoted to the breed and its well-being. New owners should have little problem finding a reputable breeder who doesn't live on the other side of the country (or in a different country). The American Kennel Club is able to recommend breeders of quality Great Pyrenees, as can any local all-breed club or Great Pyrenees club.

FINDING A QUALIFIED BREEDER

Before you begin your puppy search, ask for references from your veterinarian and perhaps other breeders to refer you to someone they believe is reputable. Responsible breeders usually raise only one or two breeds of dog. Avoid any breeder who has several different breeds or has several litters at the same time. Dedicated breeders are usually involved with a breed or other dog club. Many participate in some sport or activity related to their breed. Just as you want to be assured of the breeder's qualifications, the breeder wants to be assured that you will make a worthy owner. Expect the breeder to interview you, asking questions about your goals for the pup, your experience with dogs and what kind of home you will provide.

Once you have contacted and met a breeder or two and made your choice about which breeder is best suited to your needs, it's time to visit the litter. Keep in mind that many top breeders have waiting lists. Sometimes new owners have to wait as long as two years for a puppy. If you are really committed to the breeder whom you've selected, then you will wait (and hope for an early arrival!). If not, you may have to resort to your second- or third-choice breeder. Don't be too anxious, however. If the breeder doesn't have a waiting list, or any customers, there is probably a good reason. It's no different from visiting a restaurant with no clientele. The better restaurants always have waiting lists—and it's usually worth the wait. Besides, isn't a puppy more important than a good steak?

Breeders commonly allow visitors to see their litters by around the fifth or sixth week, and puppies leave for their new

Besides the eventual size difference between the male and female, there are other temperamental and behavioral differences to consider. Discuss sex with your chosen breeder.

homes between the eighth and tenth week. Breeders who permit their puppies to leave early are more interested in your money than in their puppies' well-being. Puppies need to learn the rules of the pack from their dams, and most dams continue teaching the pups manners and dos and don'ts until around the eighth week. Breeders spend significant amounts of time with the Great Pyrenees toddlers so that the pups are able to interact with the "other species," i.e., humans. Given the long history that dogs and humans share, bonding between the two species is natural but must be nurtured. A well-bred, well-socialized Great Pyrenees pup wants nothing more than to be near you and please you.

It is not uncommon for a breeder to have more than one litter in his kennel at one time. These 9-week-old puppies have bonded with this 16-week-old pup. Consider the advantages of acquiring a slightly older puppy that is likely house-trained and more predictable.

A COMMITTED NEW OWNER
By now you should understand what makes the Great Pyrenees a

> ### SELECTING FROM THE LITTER
> Before you visit a litter of puppies, promise yourself that you won't fall for the first pretty face you see! Decide on your goals for your puppy—show prospect, hunting dog, obedience competitor, family companion—and then look for a puppy who displays the appropriate qualities. In most litters, there is an Alpha pup (the bossy puppy), and occasionally a shy fellow who is less confident, with the rest of the litter falling somewhere in the middle. "Middle-of-the-roaders" are safe bets for most families and novice competitors.

most unique and special dog, one that will fit nicely into your family and lifestyle. If you have researched breeders, you should be able to recognize a knowledge-able and responsible Great Pyrenees breeder who cares not only about his pups but also about what kind of owner you will be. If you have completed the final step in your new journey, you have found a litter, or possibly two, of quality Great Pyrenees pups.

A visit with the puppies and their breeder should be an education in itself. Breed research, breeder selection and puppy visitation are very important aspects of finding the puppy of your dreams. Beyond that, these things also lay the

foundation for a successful future with your pup. Puppy personalities within each litter vary, from the shy and easygoing puppy to the one who is dominant and assertive, with most pups falling somewhere in between. By spending time with the puppies, you will be able to recognize certain behaviors and what these behaviors indicate about each pup's temperament. Which type of pup will complement your family dynamics is best determined by observing the puppies in action within their "pack." Your breeder's expertise and recommendations are also valuable. Although you may fall in love with a bold and brassy male, the breeder may suggest that another pup would be best for you. The breeder's experience in rearing Great Pyrenees pups and matching their temperaments with appropriate humans offers the best assurance that your pup will meet your needs and expectations. The type of puppy that you select is just as important as your decision that the Great Pyrenees is the breed for you.

The decision to live with a Great Pyrenees is a serious commitment and not one to be taken lightly. This puppy is a living sentient being that will be dependent on you for basic survival for his entire life. Beyond the basics of survival—food, water, shelter and protection—he

NEW RELEASES
Most breeders release their puppies between seven to ten weeks of age. A breeder who allows puppies to leave the litter at five or six weeks of age may be more concerned with profit than with the puppies' welfare. However, some breeders of show or working breeds may hold one or more top-quality puppies longer, occasionally until three or four months of age, in order to evaluate the puppy's career or show potential and decide which one(s) they will keep for themselves.

needs much, much more. The new pup needs love, nurturing and a proper canine education to mold him into a responsible, well-behaved canine citizen. Your Great Pyrenees's health and good manners will need consistent monitoring and regular "tune-ups." So your job as a responsible dog owner will be ongoing

MEET AND MINGLE

Puppies need to meet people and see the world if they are to grow up confident and unafraid. Take your puppy with you on everyday outings and errands. On-lead walks around the neighborhood and to the park offer the pup good exposure to the goings-on of his new human world. Avoid areas frequented by other dogs until your puppy has had his full round of puppy shots; ask your vet when your pup will be properly protected. Arrange for your puppy to meet new people of all ages every week.

throughout every stage of his life. If you are not prepared to accept these responsibilities and commit to them for the next decade, likely longer, then you are not prepared to own a dog of any breed.

Although the responsibilities of owning a dog may at times tax your patience, the joy of living with your Great Pyrenees far outweighs the workload, and a well-mannered adult dog is worth your time and effort. Before your very eyes, your new charge will grow up to be your most loyal friend, devoted to you unconditionally.

YOUR GREAT PYRENEES SHOPPING LIST

Just as expectant parents prepare a nursery for their baby, so should you ready your home for the arrival of your Great Pyrenees pup. If you have the necessary puppy supplies purchased and in place before he comes home, it will ease the puppy's transition from the warmth and familiarity of his mom and littermates to the brand-new environment of his new home and human family. You will be too busy to stock up and prepare your house after your pup comes home, that's for sure! Imagine how a pup must feel upon being transported to a strange new place. It's up to you to comfort him and to let your little pup know that he is going to be happy with you!

FOOD AND WATER BOWLS

Your puppy will need separate bowls for his food and water. Stainless steel pans are generally preferred to plastic bowls, since they sterilize better and pups are less inclined to chew on the metal. Heavy-duty ceramic bowls are popular, but consider how often you will have to pick up those heavy bowls! Buy adult-sized pans, as your puppy will grow into them before you know it.

THE DOG CRATE

If you think that crates are tools of punishment and confinement when a dog has misbehaved, think again. Most breeders and almost all trainers recommend a crate as the preferred house-training aid as well as for all-

around puppy training and safety. Because dogs are natural den creatures that prefer cave-like environments, the benefits of crate use are many. The crate provides the puppy with his very own "safe house," a cozy place to sleep, take a break or seek comfort with a favorite toy; a travel aid to house your dog when on the road, at motels or at the vet's office; a training aid to help teach your puppy proper toileting habits; a place of solitude when non-dog people happen to drop by and don't want a lively puppy...or even a well-behaved adult dog...saying hello or begging for attention.

Crates come in several types, although the wire crate and the fiberglass airline-type crate are the most

To introduce a new Great Pyrenees puppy into a household that contains older resident dogs, supervision, control and encouragement will be required to keep all family members content and comfortable.

Bowls are available in attractive pottery types or sensible stainless steel.

Your local pet shop will have a variety of crates, but the store will usually have to order one large enough for a full-grown Great Pyrenees.

Pyrenees will be a wee fellow when you bring him home, he will grow up in the blink of an eye and your puppy crate will be useless. Purchase a crate that will accommodate an adult Great Pyrenees. He will stand over 2 feet tall when full grown, so an extra-large-sized crate will fit him nicely.

BEDDING AND CRATE PADS

Your puppy will enjoy some type of soft bedding in his "room" (the crate), something he can snuggle into to feel cozy and secure. Old towels or blankets are good choices for a young pup, since he may (and probably will) have a toileting accident or two in the crate or decide to chew on the bedding material. Once he is fully trained and out of the early chewing stage, you can replace the puppy bedding with a permanent crate pad if you prefer.

popular. Both are safe and your puppy will adjust to either one, so the choice is up to you. The wire crates offer better visibility for the pup as well as better ventilation. Many of the wire crates easily collapse into suitcase-size carriers. The fiberglass crates, similar to those used by the airlines for animal transport, are sturdier and more den-like. However, the fiberglass crates do not collapse and are less ventilated than a wire crate, which can be problematic in hot weather. Some of the newer crates are made of heavy plastic mesh; these are very lightweight and fold up into slim-line suitcases. However, a mesh crate might not be suitable for a pup with manic chewing habits.

Don't bother with a puppy-sized crate. Although your Great

WHAT SIZE IS THE RIGHT SIZE?

When purchasing a crate, buy one that will fit an adult-size dog. Puppy crates are poor investments, since puppies quickly outgrow them. The crate should accommodate an adult dog in a standing position, so that he has room to stand up, turn around and lie down comfortably. A larger crate is fine but not necessary for the puppy's comfort, as most of his crate time will be spent lying down and napping.

CRATE EXPECTATIONS

To make the crate more inviting to your puppy, you can offer his first meal or two inside the crate, always keeping the crate door open so that he does not feel confined. Keep a favorite toy or two in the crate for him to play with while inside. You can also cover the crate at night with a lightweight sheet to make it more den-like and remove the stimuli of household activity. Never put him into his crate as punishment or as you are scolding him, since he will then associate his crate with negative situations and avoid going there.

Crate pads and other dog beds run the gamut from inexpensive to high-end doggie-designer styles, but don't splurge on the good stuff until you are sure that your puppy is reliable and won't tear it up or make a mess on it.

PUPPY TOYS

Just as infants and children require objects to stimulate their minds and bodies, puppies need toys to entertain their curious brains, wiggly paws and achy teeth. A fun array of safe doggie toys will help satisfy your puppy's chewing instincts and distract him from gnawing on the leg of your antique chair or your new leather sofa. Most puppy toys are cute and look like they would be a lot of fun, but not all are necessarily safe or good for your puppy, so use caution when you go puppy-toy shopping.

Although Great Pyrenees are not known to be voracious chewers like many other dogs, they still love to chew. The best "chewcifiers" are nylon and hard rubber bones; many are safe to gnaw on and come in sizes appropriate for all age groups and breeds. Be especially careful of natural bones, which can splinter or develop dangerous sharp edges; pups can easily swallow or choke on those bone splinters. Veterinarians often tell of surgical

Treats are great rewards for the well-behaved puppy.

Many breeders will acclimate the litter to exercise pens and crates as a part of the pups' basic education. Puppies that are accustomed to being confined will more readily accept crate training in their new homes.

nightmares involving bits of splintered bone, because in addition to the danger of choking, the sharp pieces can damage the intestinal tract.

Similarly, rawhide chews, while a favorite of most dogs and puppies, can be equally dangerous. Pieces of rawhide are easily swallowed after they get all gummy from chewing, and dogs have been known to choke on large pieces of ingested rawhide. Rawhide chews should be offered only when you can supervise the puppy.

Soft woolly toys are special puppy favorites. They come in a wide variety of cute shapes and sizes; some look like little stuffed animals. Puppies love to shake them up and toss them about, or simply carry them around. Be careful of fuzzy toys that have button eyes or noses that your pup could chew off and swallow, and make sure that he does not "disembowel" a squeaky toy to remove the squeaker! Braided rope toys are similar in that they are fun to chew and toss around, but they shred easily and the strings are easy to swallow. The strings are not digestible and, if the puppy doesn't pass them in his stool, he could end up at the vet's office. As with rawhides, your puppy should be closely monitored with rope toys.

If you believe that your pup has ingested one of these forbidden objects, check his stools for the next couple of days to see if he passes them when he defecates. At the same time, also watch for signs of intestinal distress. A call to your veterinarian might be in order to get his advice and be on the safe side.

An all-time favorite toy for puppies (young and old!) is the

GOOD CHEWING

Chew toys run the gamut from rawhide chews to hard sterile bones and everything in between. Rawhides are all-time favorites, but they can cause choking when they become mushy from repeated chewing, causing them to break into small pieces that are easy to swallow. Rawhides are also highly indigestible, so many vets advise limiting rawhide treats. Hard sterile bones are great for plaque prevention as well as chewing satisfaction. Dispose of them when the ends become sharp or splintered.

empty gallon milk jug. Hard plastic juice containers – 46 ounces or more – are also excellent. Such containers make lots of noise when they are batted about and puppies go crazy with delight as they play with them. However, they don't often last very long, so be sure to remove and replace them when they get chewed up on the ends.

A word of caution about homemade toys: be careful with your choices of non-traditional play objects. Never use old shoes or socks, since a puppy cannot distinguish between the old ones on which he's allowed to chew and the new ones in your closet that are strictly off limits. That principle applies to anything that resembles something that you don't want your puppy to chew up.

COLLARS

A lightweight nylon collar is the best choice for a very young pup. Quick-clip collars are easy to put on and remove, and they can be adjusted as the puppy grows. Introduce him to his collar as soon as he comes home to get him accustomed to wearing it. He'll get used to it quickly and won't mind a bit. Make sure that it is snug enough that it won't slip off, yet loose enough to be comfortable for the pup. You should be able to slip two fingers between the collar and his neck.

TOYS 'R SAFE

The vast array of tantalizing puppy toys is staggering. Stroll through any pet shop or pet-supply outlet and you will see that the choices can be overwhelming. However, not all dog toys are safe or sensible. Most very young puppies enjoy soft woolly toys that they can snuggle with and carry around. (You know they have outgrown them when they shred them up!) Avoid toys that have buttons, tabs or other enhancements that can be chewed off and swallowed. Soft toys that squeak are fun, but make sure your puppy does not disembowel the toy and remove (and swallow) the squeaker. Toys that rattle or make noise can excite a puppy, but they present the same danger as the squeaky kind and so require supervision. Hard rubber toys that bounce can also entertain a pup, but make sure the size of the toy is too big to swallow.

Your local pet
shop will have a
wide array of
leads suitable for
your Great
Pyrenees.

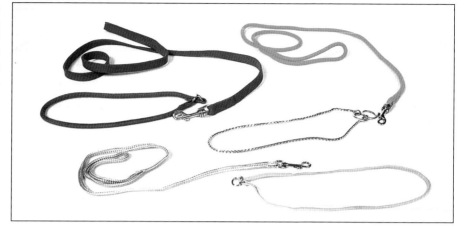

Check the collar often, as puppies grow in spurts and his collar can become too tight almost overnight. Choke collars are for training purposes only and should never be used on a puppy under four or five months old.

LEASHES
A 6-foot nylon lead is an excellent choice for a young puppy. It is lightweight and not as tempting to chew as a leather lead. You can switch to a 6-foot leather lead after your pup has grown and is used to walking politely on a lead. For initial puppy walks and house-training purposes, you should invest in a shorter lead so that you have more control over the puppy. At first, you don't want him wandering too far away from you, and when taking him out for toileting you will want to keep him in the specific area chosen

for his potty spot.

Once the puppy is heel trained with a traditional leash, you can consider purchasing a retractable lead. A flexible lead is excellent for walking adult dogs that are already leash-wise. The "flexi" allows the dog to roam farther away from you and explore a wider area when out walking, and also retracts when you need to keep him close to you.

COST OF OWNERSHIP
The purchase price of your puppy is merely the first expense in the typical dog budget. Quality dog food, veterinary care (sickness and health maintenance), dog supplies and grooming costs will add up to big bucks every year. Can you adequately afford to support a canine addition to the family?

COLLARING OUR CANINES

The standard flat collar with a buckle or a snap, in leather, nylon or cotton, is widely regarded as the everyday all-purpose collar. If the collar fits correctly, you should be able to fit two fingers between the collar and the dog's neck. Such a flat collar is suitable for most breeds of dogs, but greyhound-like dogs (with slender skulls and necks) and thick-necked dogs can easily back out of a collar.

Leather Buckle Collars

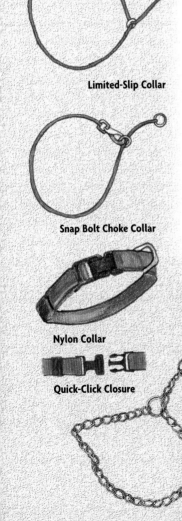

Limited-Slip Collar

Snap Bolt Choke Collar

Nylon Collar

Quick-Click Closure

The martingale, greyhound or limited-slip collar is preferred by many dog owners and trainers. It is fixed with an extra loop that tightens when pressure is applied to the leash. The martingale collar gets tighter but does not "choke" the dog. The limited-slip collar should only be used for walking and training, not for free play or interaction with another dog. These types of collar should never be left on the dog, as the extra loop can lead to accidents.

Choke collars, usually made of stainless steel, are made for training purposes, though are not recommended for small dogs or heavily coated breeds. The chains can injure small dogs or damage long/abundant coats. Thin nylon choke leads are commonly used on show dogs while in the ring, though these are not practical for everyday use.

The harness, with two or three straps that attach over the dog's shoulders and around his torso, is a humane and safe alternative to the conventional collar. By and large, a well-made harness is virtually escape-proof. Harnesses are available in nylon and mesh and can be outfitted on most dogs, ranging from chest girths of 10 to 30 inches.

Harness

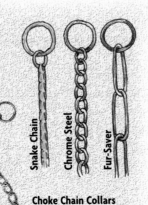

Snake Chain

Chrome Steel

Fur-Saver

Choke Chain Collars

A head collar, composed of a nylon strap that goes around the dog's muzzle and a second strap that wraps around his neck, offers the owner better control over his dog. This device is recommended for problem-solving with dogs (including jumping up, pulling and aggressive behaviors), but must be used with care.

A training halter, including a flat collar and two straps, made of nylon and webbing, is designed for walking. There are several on the market; some are more difficult to put on the dog than others. The halter harness, with two small slip rings at each end, is recommended for ease of use.

A Dog-Safe Home

The dog-safety police are taking you and your new puppy on a house tour. Let's go room by room and see how safe your own home is for your new pup. The following items are doggie dangers, so either they must be removed or the dog should be monitored or not have access to these areas.

Living Room
- house plants (some varieties are poisonous)
- fireplace or wood-burning stove
- paint on the walls (lead-based paint is toxic)
- lead drapery weights (toxic lead)
- lamps and electrical cords
- carpet cleaners or deodorizers

Outdoor
- swimming pool
- pesticides
- toxic plants
- lawn fertilizers

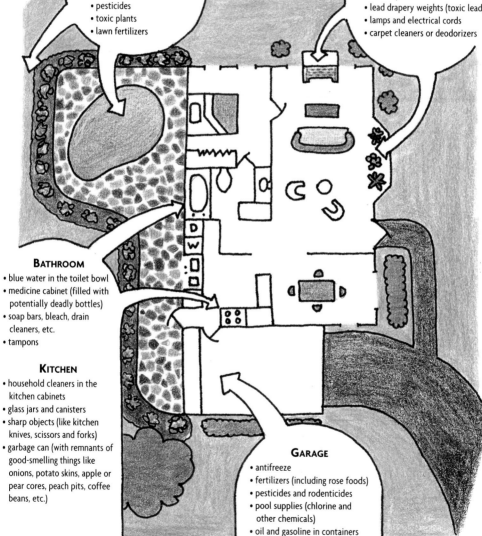

Bathroom
- blue water in the toilet bowl
- medicine cabinet (filled with potentially deadly bottles)
- soap bars, bleach, drain cleaners, etc.
- tampons

Kitchen
- household cleaners in the kitchen cabinets
- glass jars and canisters
- sharp objects (like kitchen knives, scissors and forks)
- garbage can (with remnants of good-smelling things like onions, potato skins, apple or pear cores, peach pits, coffee beans, etc.)

Garage
- antifreeze
- fertilizers (including rose foods)
- pesticides and rodenticides
- pool supplies (chlorine and other chemicals)
- oil and gasoline in containers
- sharp objects, electrical cords and power tools

HOME SAFETY FOR YOUR PUPPY

The importance of puppy-proofing cannot be overstated. In addition to making your house comfortable for your Great Pyrenees's arrival, you also must make sure that your house is safe for your puppy before you bring him home. There are countless hazards in the owner's personal living environment that a pup can sniff, chew, swallow or destroy. Many are obvious; others are not. Do a thorough advance house check to remove or rearrange those things that could hurt your puppy, keeping any potentially dangerous items out of areas to which he will have access.

Electrical cords are especially dangerous, since puppies view them as irresistible chew toys. Unplug and remove all exposed cords or fasten them beneath a baseboard where the puppy cannot reach them. Veterinarians and firefighters can tell you horror stories about electrical burns and house fires that resulted from puppy-chewed electrical cords. Consider this a most serious precaution for your puppy and the rest of your family.

Scout your home for tiny objects that might be seen at a pup's eye level. Keep medication bottles and cleaning supplies well out of reach, and do the same with waste baskets and other trash containers. It goes without saying that you should not use rodent poison or other toxic chemicals in any puppy area and that you must keep such containers safely locked up. You will be amazed at how many places a curious puppy can discover!

Once your house has cleared inspection, check your yard. A sturdy fence, well embedded into the ground, will give your dog a safe place to play and potty. Although Great Pyrenees are not known to be climbers or fence jumpers, they are still athletic

FIRST CAR RIDE

The ride to your home from the breeder will no doubt be your puppy's first automobile experience, and you should make every effort to keep him comfortable and secure. Bring a large towel or small blanket for the puppy to lie on during the trip, and an extra towel in case the pup gets carsick or has a potty accident. It's best to have another person with you to hold the puppy in his lap. Most puppies will fall fast asleep from the rolling motion of the car. If the ride is lengthy, your may have to stop so that the puppy can relieve himself, so be sure to bring a leash and collar for those stops. Avoid rest areas for potty trips, since those are frequented by many dogs, who may carry parasites or disease. It's better to stop at grassy areas near gas stations or shopping centers to prevent unhealthy exposure for your pup.

DIGGING OUT

Some dogs love to dig. Others wouldn't think of it. Digging is considered "self-rewarding behavior" because it's fun! Of all the digging solutions offered by the experts, most are only marginally successful and none is guaranteed to work. The best cure is prevention, which means removing the dog from the offending site when he digs as well as distracting him when you catch him digging so that he turns his attentions elsewhere. That means that you have to supervise your dog's yard time. An unsupervised digger can create havoc with your landscaping, or worse, run away!

dogs, so a 5- to 6-foot-high fence should be adequate to contain an agile youngster or adult. Check the fence periodically for necessary repairs. If there is a weak link or space to squeeze through, you can be sure a determined Great Pyrenees will discover it.

The garage and shed can be hazardous places for a pup, as things like fertilizers, chemicals and tools are usually kept there. It's best to keep these areas off-limits to the pup. Antifreeze is especially dangerous to dogs, as they find the taste appealing, and it only takes a few licks from the driveway to kill a dog, puppy or adult.

VISITING THE VETERINARIAN

A good veterinarian is your Great Pyrenees puppy's best health insurance policy. If you do not already have a vet, ask friends and experienced dog people in your area for recommendations so that you can select a vet before you bring your Great Pyrenees puppy home. Also arrange for your puppy's first veterinary examination beforehand, since many vets have two- and three-week waiting periods, and your puppy should visit the vet within a day or so of coming home.

It's important to make sure your puppy's first visit to the vet is a pleasant and positive one. The vet should take great care to befriend the pup and handle him gently to make their first meeting a positive experience. The vet will give the pup a thorough physical examination and set up a schedule for vaccinations and other necessary wellness visits. Be sure to show your vet any health and inoculation records, which you should have received from

PUPPY SHOTS

Puppies are born with natural antibodies that protect them from most canine diseases. They receive more antibodies from the colostrum in their mother's milk. These immunities wear off, however, and must be replaced through a series of vaccines. Puppy shots are given at 3- to 4-week intervals starting at 6 to 8 weeks of age through 12 to 16 weeks of age. Booster shots are given after one year of age, and every one to three years thereafter.

Despite his fuzzy wagging tail, he is still apprehensive and wondering where he is and who all these strange humans are. It's best to let him explore on his own and meet the family members as he feels comfortable. Let him investigate all the new smells, sights and sounds at his own pace. Children should be especially careful to not get overly excited, use loud voices or hug the pup too tightly. Be calm, gentle and affectionate, and be ready to comfort him if he appears

your breeder. Your vet is a great source of canine health information, so be sure to ask questions and take notes. Creating a health journal for your puppy will make a handy reference for his wellness and any future health problems that may arise.

MEETING THE FAMILY

Your Great Pyrenees's homecoming is an exciting time for all members of the family, and it's only natural that everyone will be eager to meet him, pet him and play with him. However, for the puppy's sake, it's best to make these initial family meetings as uneventful as possible, so that the pup is not overwhelmed with too much too soon. Remember, he has just left his dam and his littermates and is away from the breeder's home for the first time.

The arrival of your Pyrenees puppy will be an exciting time for the whole family. Do not overwhelm your new charge, and introduce him to the family in as low-key a manner as possible.

frightened or uneasy.

Be sure to show your puppy his new crate during this first day home. Toss a treat or two inside the crate; if he associates the crate with food, he will associate the crate with good things. If he is comfortable with the crate, you can offer him his first meal inside it. Leave the door ajar so he can wander in and out as he chooses.

FIRST NIGHT IN HIS NEW HOME

So much has happened in your Great Pyrenees puppy's first day away from the breeder. He's had his first car ride to his new home. He's met his new human family and perhaps the other family pets. He has explored his new house and yard, at least those places where he is to be allowed during his first weeks at home. He may have visited his new veterinarian. He has eaten his first meal or two away from his dam and litter-mates. Surely that's enough to tire out an eight-week-old Great Pyrenees pup…or so you hope!

It's bedtime. During the day, the pup investigated his crate, which is his new den and sleeping space, so it is not entirely strange to him. Line the crate with a soft towel or blanket that he can snuggle into and gently place him into the crate for the night. Some breeders send home a piece of bedding from where the pup slept with his littermates, and those familiar scents are a great comfort for the puppy on his first night without his siblings.

He will probably whine or cry. The puppy is objecting to the confinement and the fact that he is alone for the first time. This can be a stressful time for you as well as for the pup. It's important that you remain strong and don't let the puppy out of his crate to comfort him. He will fall asleep eventually. If you release him, the puppy will learn that crying means "out" and will continue that habit. You are laying the groundwork for future habits.

THE FIRST FAMILY MEETING
Your puppy's first day at home should be quiet and uneventful. Despite his wagging tail, he is still wondering where his mom and siblings are! Let him make friends with other members of the family on his own terms; don't overwhelm him. You have a lifetime ahead to get to know each other!

Some breeders find that soft music can soothe a crying pup and help him get to sleep.

SOCIALIZING YOUR PUPPY

The next 20 weeks of your Great Pyrenees puppy's life are the most important of his entire lifetime. A properly socialized puppy will grow up to be a confident and stable adult who will be a pleasure to live with and a welcome addition to the neighborhood.

The importance of socialization cannot be overemphasized. Research on canine behavior has proven that puppies who are not exposed to new sights, sounds, people and animals during their first 20 weeks of life will grow up to be timid and fearful, even aggressive, and unable to flourish outside of their home environment

Socializing your puppy is not difficult and, in fact, will be a fun time for you both. Lead training goes hand in hand with socialization, so your puppy will be learning how to walk on a lead at the same time that he's meeting the neighborhood. Because the Great Pyrenees is a such a terrific breed, your puppy will enjoy being "the new kid on the block." Take him for short walks, to the park and to other dog-friendly places where he will encounter new people, especially children. Puppies automatically recognize

CREATE A SCHEDULE
Puppies thrive on sameness and routine. Offer meals at the same time each day, take him out at regular times for potty trips and do the same for play periods and outdoor activity. Make note of when your puppy naps and when he is most lively and energetic, and try to plan his day around those times. Once he is house-trained and more predictable in his habits, he will be better able to tolerate changes in his schedule.

children as "little people" and are drawn to play with them. Just make sure that you supervise these meetings and that the children do not get too rough or encourage him to play too hard. An overzealous pup can often nip too hard, frightening the child and in turn making the puppy overly excited. A bad experience in puppyhood can impact a dog for life; thus a pup that has a negative experience with a child may grow up to be shy or even aggressive around children.

Take your puppy along on your daily errands. Puppies are natural "people magnets" and most people who see your pup will want to pet him. All of these encounters will help to mold him into a confident adult dog. Likewise, you will soon feel like a confident, responsible dog owner, rightly proud of your handsome Great Pyrenees.

Be especially careful of your puppy's encounters and experiences during the eight-to-ten-week-old period, which is also called the "fear period." This is a serious imprinting period, and all contact during this time should be gentle and positive. A frightening or negative event could leave a permanent impression that could affect his future behavior if a similar situation arises.

Also make sure that your puppy has received his first and second rounds of vaccinations

---

THE WORRIES OF MANGE
Sometimes called "puppy mange," demodectic mange is passed to the puppy through the mother's milk. These microscopic mites take up residence in the puppy's hair follicles and sebaceous glands. Stress can cause the mites to multiply, causing bare patches on the face, neck and front legs. If neglected, it can lead to secondary bacterial infections, but if diagnosed and treated early, demodectic mange can be localized and controlled. Most pups recover without complications.

---

before you expose him to other dogs or bring him to places that other dogs may frequent. Avoid dog parks and other strange-dog areas until your vet assures you that your puppy is fully immunized and resistant to the diseases that can be passed between canines. Discuss socialization with your breeder, as some breeders recommend socializing the puppy even before he has received all his inoculations, depending on how outgoing the puppy may be.

LEADER OF THE PUPPY'S PACK

Like other canines, your puppy needs an authority figure, someone he can look up to and regard as the leader of his "pack." His first pack leader was his dam, who taught him to be polite and

The Great Pyrenees is a natural guardian and protector. Even young puppies feel the instinct to survey the property.

MAKE A COMMITMENT

Dogs are most assuredly man's best friend, but they are also a lot of work. When you add a puppy to your family, you also are adding to your daily responsibilities for the next 10 to 15 years. Dogs need more than just food, water and a place to sleep. They also require training (which can be ongoing throughout the lifetime of the dog), activity to keep him physically and mentally fit and hands-on attention every day, plus grooming and health care. Your life as you now know it may well disappear! Are you prepared for such drastic changes?

imagine your adorable Great Pyrenees puppy trying to be in charge when he is so small and seemingly helpless. You must remember that these are natural canine instincts. Do not cave in and allow your pup to get the upper "paw!"

Just as socialization is so important during these first 20 weeks, so too is your puppy's early education. He was born without any bad habits. He does not know what is good or bad behavior. If he does things like nipping and digging, it's because he is having fun and doesn't know that humans consider these things as "bad." It's your job to teach him proper puppy manners, and this is the best time to accomplish that…before he has developed bad

not chew too hard on her ears or nip at her muzzle. He learned those same lessons from his litter-mates. If he played too rough, they cried in pain and stopped the game, which sent an important message to the rowdy puppy.

As puppies play together, they are also struggling to determine who will be the boss. Being pack animals, dogs need someone to be in charge. If a litter of puppies remained together beyond puppyhood, one of the pups would emerge as the strongest one, the one who calls the shots.

Once your puppy leaves the pack, he will look intuitively for a new leader. If he does not recognize you as that leader, he will try to assume that position for himself. Of course, it is hard to

Before the puppy is released from the breeder, it should have had some exposure to young people. At the precious age of six weeks, a puppy must be supervised whenever a child is present to ensure that both are on their best behavior.

conference before your pup comes home so that everyone understands the basic principles of puppy training and the rules you have set forth for the pup, and agrees to follow them.

The old adage "an ounce of prevention is worth a pound of cure" is especially true when it comes to puppies. It is much easier to prevent inappropriate behavior than it is to change it. It's also easier and less stressful for the pup, since it will keep discipline to a minimum and create a more positive learning environment for him. That, in turn, will also be easier on you!

Here are a few common sense tips to keep your belongings safe

Your puppy learned his most important lessons from his dam. Now you have to communicate with him so that he understands your wishes.

habits, since it is much more difficult to "unlearn" or correct unacceptable learned behavior than to teach good behavior from the start.

Make sure that all members of the family understand the importance of being consistent when training their new puppy. If you tell the puppy to stay off the sofa, and your daughter allows him to cuddle on the couch to watch her favorite television show, your pup will be confused about what he is and is not allowed to do. Have a family

HOUSE-TRAINING SIGNALS

Watch your puppy for signs that he has to relieve himself (sniffing, circling and squatting), and waste no time in whisking him outside to do his business. Once the puppy is older, you should attach his leash and head for the door. Puppies will always "go" immediately after they wake up, within minutes after eating and after brief periods of play, but young puppies should also be taken out regularly at times other than these, just in case! If necessary, set a timer to remind you to take him out.

and your puppy out of trouble:

- Keep your closet doors closed and your shoes, socks and other apparel off the floor so your puppy can't get at them.
- Keep a secure lid on the trash container or put the trash where your puppy can't dig into it. He can't damage what he can't reach!
- Supervise your puppy at all times to make sure he is not getting into mischief. If he starts to chew the corner of the rug, you can distract him instantly by tossing a toy for him to fetch. You also will be able to whisk him outside when you notice that he is about to piddle on the carpet. If you can't see your puppy, you can't teach or correct his behavior.

SOLVING PUPPY PROBLEMS

CHEWING AND NIPPING

Nipping at fingers and toes is normal puppy behavior. Chewing is also the way that puppies investigate their surroundings. However, you will have to teach your puppy that chewing anything other than his toys is not acceptable. That won't happen overnight and, at times, puppy teeth will test your patience. However, if you allow nipping and chewing to continue, just think about the damage that a mature Great Pyrenees can do with a full set of adult teeth.

BE CONSISTENT

Consistency is a key element, in fact is absolutely necessary, to a puppy's learning environment. A behavior (such as chewing, jumping up or climbing onto the furniture) cannot be forbidden one day and then allowed the next. That will only confuse the pup and he will not understand what he is supposed to do. Just one or two episodes of allowing an undesirable behavior to "slide" will imprint that behavior on a puppy's brain and make that behavior more difficult to erase or change.

Whenever your puppy nips your hand or fingers, cry out "Ouch!" in a loud voice, which should startle your puppy and stop him from nipping, even if only for a moment. Immediately distract him by offering a small treat or an appropriate toy for him to chew instead (which means having chew toys and puppy treats handy or in your pockets at all times). Praise him when he takes the toy and tell him what a good fellow he is. Praise is just as, or even more, important to puppy training as discipline and correction.

Puppies also tend to nip at children more often than adults, since they perceive little ones to be more vulnerable and more similar to their littermates. Teach your children appropriate responses to nipping behavior and, if they are unable to handle it themselves, you may have to intervene. Puppy nips can be quite painful and a child's frightened reaction will only encourage a puppy to nip harder, which is a natural canine response. As with all other puppy situations, interaction between your Great Pyrenees puppy and children should be supervised.

Chewing on objects, not just family members' fingers and ankles, is also normal canine behavior that can be especially tedious (for the owner, not the pup) during the teething period when the puppy's adult teeth are coming in. At this stage, chewing

There's no clearer method of saying "good job" than a tasty liver treat.

just plain feels good. Furniture legs and cabinet corners are common puppy favorites. Shoes and other personal items also taste pretty good to a pup.

The best solution is, once again, prevention. If you value something, keep it tucked away and out of reach. You can't hide your dining-room table in a closet, but you can try to deflect the chewing by applying a bitter product made just to deter dogs from chewing. Available in a spray or cream, this substance is vile-tasting, although safe for dogs, and most puppies will avoid the forbidden object after one tiny taste. You also can apply the product to your leather leash if the puppy tries to chew on his lead during leash- training sessions.

Keep a ready supply of safe chews handy to offer your Great Pyrenees as a distraction when he starts to chew on something that's a "no-no." Remember, at this tender age, he does not yet know what is permitted or forbidden, so you have to be "on call" every minute he's awake and on the prowl.

You may lose a treasure or two during puppy's growing-up period, and the furniture could sustain a nasty nick or two. These can be trying times, so be prepared for those inevitable accidents and comfort yourself in knowing that this too shall pass.

PUPPY WHINING

Puppies often cry and whine, just as infants and little children do. It's their way of telling us that they are lonely or in need of attention. Your puppy will miss his littermates and will feel insecure when he is left alone. You may be out of the house or just in another room, but he will still feel alone. During these times, the puppy's crate should be his personal comfort station, a place all his own where he can feel safe and secure. Once he learns that being alone is okay and not something to be feared, he will settle down without crying or objecting. You might want to leave a radio on while he is crated, as the sound of human voices can be soothing and will give the impression that people are around.

Give your puppy a favorite cuddly toy or chew toy to entertain him whenever he is crated. You will both be happier: the puppy because he is safe in his den and you because he is quiet, safe and not getting into puppy escapades that can wreak havoc in your house or cause him danger.

To make sure that your puppy will always view his crate as a safe and cozy place, never, ever, use the crate as punishment. That's the best way to turn the crate into a negative place that the pup will want to avoid. Sure, you can use the crate for your own peace of mind if your puppy is getting into trouble and needs some "time out." Just don't let him know that! Never scold the pup and immediately place him in the crate. Count to ten, give him a couple of hugs and maybe a treat, then scoot him into his crate.

It's also important not to make a big fuss when he is released from the crate. That will make getting out of the crate more appealing than being in the crate, which is just the opposite of what you are trying to achieve.

Puppies that are left alone for long periods can suffer from separation anxiety, punctuated by whining, pouting and alarmingly sad expressions.

PROPER CARE OF YOUR

GREAT PYRENEES

FEEDING THE PYRENEES

A Great Pyrenees should be fed sensibly on a high-quality diet, but protein content will vary according to whether or not the dog lives an especially active lifestyle. When purchasing a puppy, a carefully selected breeder should be able to give good advice in this regard, but it is generally accepted that dogs leading active lives need more protein than those who spend most of their time by the fireside.

It is difficult to over-feed a Pyrenees puppy, for they get the sensation of feeling full quite quickly. This is not a greedy breed; Pyrenees, in general, tend to eat less in quantity than might be expected for their size. However, correct feeding is very important, especially during the crucial stage of bone growth.

Although Pyrenees are not especially susceptible to excess weight gain, an owner should never be tempted to allow a dog to put on too much weight. An overweight dog is more prone to health problems than one that is of correct weight for its size. Feeding any dog tidbits between meals will run the

risk of having an unhealthy, overweight dog in maturity.

There are now numerous high-quality canine meals available, and one of them is sure to suit your own Great Pyrenees. Once again, you should be able to obtain sound advice from your dog's breeder as to which food is considered most suitable. Whether or not you decide to feed a small amount of extra calcium will depend largely on the diet you have chosen; discuss this with your vet. When you buy your puppy, the breeder should provide you with a diet sheet that gives details of exactly how your puppy has been fed. Of course you will be at liberty to change that food,

A well-cared-for Great Pyrenees puppy is a happy, smiling companion.

Facing page: Along with the allure and dignity of the Great Pyrenees comes a great deal of responsibility.

Your new Pyrenees puppy should be offered the same high-quality food that the breeder offered. Should you decide to change the brand, do so very gradually so as not to upset the puppy's system.

together with the frequency and timing of meals, as the youngster reaches adulthood, but this should be done gradually.

Some owners still prefer to feed fresh food, instead of one of the more convenient complete diets. However, there are so many of the latter now available, some scientifically balanced, that a lot will depend on personal preference. If you have a 'finicky eater,' although you have to be very careful not to unbalance an otherwise balanced diet, sometimes a little added fresh meat, or even beef or chicken

stock, will gain a dog's interest and stimulate the appetite.

TYPES OF FOOD AND READING THE LABEL

When selecting the type of food to feed your dog, it is important to check out the label for ingredients. Many dry-food products have soybean, corn or rice as the main ingredient. The main ingredient will be listed first on the label, with the rest of the ingredients following in descending order according to their proportion in the food. While these types of dry food are fine, you should also look into dry foods based on meat or fish. These are better-quality foods and thus higher priced. However, they may be just as economical in the long run, because studies have shown that it takes a smaller quantity of the higher-quality foods to maintain a dog.

Comparing the various types of food, dry, canned and semi-moist, dry foods contain the least amount of water whereas canned foods contain the most water. Proportionately, dry foods are the most calorie- and nutrient-dense, which means that you need more of a canned food product to supply the same amount of nutrition. For Great Pyrenees, this can be an issue, since it takes a large volume of canned food to fulfill their nutritional needs. Small breeds do fine on canned

foods and, if feeding dry food to a small dog, it is wise to choose a "small bite" formula with pieces that are easier for their small mouths and teeth to handle. So, while the choice of food type is an individual one based on owner preference and what the dog seems to like, think canned for the small guys and dry or semi-moist for larger breeds. You may find success mixing the food types as well. Water is important for all dogs, but even more so for those fed dry foods, as there is not a high water content in their food.

There are strict controls that regulate the nutritional content of dog food, and a food has to meet the minimum requirements in order to be considered "complete and balanced." It is important that you choose such a food for your dog, so check the label to be sure that your chosen food meets the requirements. If not, look for a food that clearly states on the label that it is formulated to be complete and balanced for your

Most breeders recommend feeding dry food to their Pyrs, though canned food can be used for one meal.

JUST ADD MEAT

An organic alternative to the traditional dog kibble or canned food comes in the form of grain-based feeds. These dry cereal-type products consist of oat and rye flakes, corn meal, wheat germ, dried kelp and other natural ingredients. The manufacturers recommend that the food be mixed with raw meat in a ratio of two parts grain to one part meat. As an alternative to fresh meat, investigate freeze-dried meat and fermented meat products, which makers claim are more nutritious and digestible for dogs.

dog's particular stage of life.

Recommendations for amounts to feed will also be indicated on the label. You should also ask your vet about proper food portions, and you will keep an eye on your dog's condition to see if the recommended amounts are adequate. If he becomes over- or underweight, you will need to make adjustments and this also would be a good time to consult your vet.

QUICKLY FEELING FULL

Perhaps surprisingly, it is difficult to over-feed a Great Pyrenees puppy. They seem to feel full quite quickly. If feeding fresh meat in their diet, this breed seems especially to like tripe, for to eat the stomach and intestines is quite natural for them.

The food label may also make feeding suggestions, such as if moistening a dry-food product is recommended. Sometimes a splash of water will make the food more palatable for the dog and even enhance the flavor. Don't be overwhelmed by the many factors that go into feeding your dog. Manufacturers of complete and balanced foods make it easy, and once you find the right food and amounts for your own dog, his daily feeding will be a matter of routine.

DON'T FORGET THE WATER!

For a dog, it's always time for a drink! Regardless of what type of food he eats, there's no doubt that he needs plenty of water. Fresh cold water, in a clean bowl, should be freely available to your dog at all times. There are special circumstances, such as during puppy housebreaking, when you will want to monitor your pup's water intake so that you will be able to predict when he will need to relieve himself, but water must be available to him nonetheless. Water is essential for hydration and proper body function just as it is in humans.

You will get to know how much your dog typically drinks in a day. Of course, in the heat or if exercising vigorously, he will be more thirsty and will drink more. However, if he begins to drink noticeably more water for no

QUENCHING HIS THIRST

Is your dog drinking more than normal and trying to lap up everything in sight? Excessive drinking has so many different causes. Obvious causes for a dog's being thirstier than usual are hot weather and vigorous exercise. However, if your dog is drinking more for no apparent reason, you could have cause for concern. Serious conditions like kidney or liver disease, diabetes and various types of hormonal problems can all be indicated by excessive drinking. If you notice your dog's being excessively thirsty, contact your vet at once. Hopefully there will be a simpler explanation, but the earlier a serious problem is detected, the sooner it can be treated, with a better rate of cure.

apparent reason, this could signal any of various problems, and you are advised to consult your vet.

Water is the best drink for dogs. Some owners are tempted to give milk from time to time or to moisten dry food with milk, but dogs do not have the enzymes necessary to digest the lactose in milk, which is much different from the milk that nursing puppies receive. Therefore stick with clean fresh water to quench your dog's thirst, and always have it readily available to him.

A word of caution concerning your deep-chested dog's water intake: he should never be allowed to gulp water, especially at mealtimes. In fact, his water intake should be limited at mealtimes as a rule. This simple daily precaution can go a long way in protecting your dog from the dangerous and potentially fatal gastric torsion (bloat).

SPECIAL FEEDING CONSIDERATIONS

Pregnancy and Lactation: To start, a breeding female should be in good bodily condition. To maintain good condition during pregnancy, it is important to consider her individual factors, such as age, metabolism and activity level.

The gestation period is roughly nine weeks, and during the first two trimesters a pregnant bitch's nutrition needs are the same as her regular maintenance diet. However, during the last two or three weeks, her requirements increase for all nutrients; this can be achieved by increasing her food

These two pups are quickly outgrowing their bowl.

intake and making sure she is getting enough protein. As there are foods manufactured for all life stages, there are complete and balanced foods formulated for pregnant bitches. With this type of food, supplementation is not necessary, and too-high levels of certain nutrients can cause problems.

The pregnant female's appetite can fluctuate during pregnancy. At some point she may seem less interested in food but will tend to eat more in the later weeks. This is normal and should not be a concern unless she begins to lose condition. In this case, she must be encouraged to eat, perhaps enticing her with moist food or a different flavor, to keep up her strength and weight. As whelping approaches, again she may lose her appetite, but this is often a sign that the puppies are on their way within the next day or two.

As with any stage of life, water is essential. In pregnancy, it plays the additional role of delivering nutrients to the developing puppies and helping milk production, along with keeping the female in good condition herself.

Milk production is an extra-demanding life stage in terms of nutrition. Her needs can be met with a complete and balanced dog food formulated for reproduction and growth (the same food used during pregnancy is fine), fed in larger amounts than her maintenance diet. This continues for about four weeks after whelping. She may eat as much as four times her normal portion, and she should be allowed as much food as she wants. Proportionate to her increased food intake and to help with milk production, her water needs will increase as well.

As the puppies are weaned, your vet will advise you of dietary changes to aid the dam in slowing milk production and resuming a normal diet.

Working and Very Active Dogs: The more a dog does, the more he needs to eat! Examples of dogs with higher nutrient requirements are dogs who are very active in training for or competing in sporting disciplines and dogs that are used in a working capacity such as herding or hunting. They do not need supplementation to their regular food; rather, because they need larger amounts of all nutrients, they will need their maintenance

Young puppies should not be overfed, as this can contribute to orthopedic problems later in life.

WHAT IS "BLOAT"?

Need yet another reason to avoid tossing your dog a morsel from your plate? It is shown that dogs fed table scraps have an increased risk of developing bloat or gastric torsion. Did you know that more occurrences of bloat occur in the warm-weather months due to the frequency of outdoor cooking and dining, and dogs' receiving "samples" from the fired-up Weber®.

You likely have heard the term "bloat," which refers to gastric torsion (gastric dilatation/volvulus), a potentially fatal condition. As it is directly related to feeding and exercise practices, a brief explanation here is warranted. The term *dilatation* means that the dog's stomach is filled with air, while *volvulus* means that the stomach is twisted around on itself, blocking the entrance/exit points. Dilatation/volvulus is truly a deadly combination, although they also can occur independently of each other. An affected dog cannot digest food or pass gas, and blood cannot flow to the stomach, causing accumulation of toxins and gas, great pain and shock.

Many theories exist on what exactly causes bloat, but we do know that deep-chested breeds are more prone. Activities like eating a large meal, gulping water, strenuous exercise too close to mealtimes or a combination of these can contribute to bloat, though not every case is directly related to these more well-known causes. With that in mind, we can focus on incorporating simple daily preventatives and knowing how to recognize the symptoms. Affected dogs need immediate veterinary attention, as death can result quickly. Signs include obvious restlessness/discomfort, crying in pain, drooling/excessive salivation, unproductive attempts to vomit or relieve himself, visibly bloated appearance and collapsing. Do not wait: get to the vet right away if you see any of these symptoms. The vet will confirm by X-ray if the stomach is bloated with air; if so, the dog must be treated *immediately*.

A bloated dog will be treated for shock, and the stomach must be relieved of the air pressure as well as surgically returned to its correct position. If part of the stomach wall has died, that part must be removed. Usually the stomach is stapled to the abdominal wall to prevent another episode of bloating; this may or may not be successful. The vet should also check the dog for heart problems related to the condition.

Clean, fresh water is an essential part of your Great Pyrenees' diet!

food in larger portions. Also ask your vet about specially formulated "performance" diets for active dogs.

When feeding an active dog, it is essential to provide adequate periods of rest before and after eating to avoid stomach upset or the more serious gastric torsion, which can be fatal. Treats can be fed during rest periods as well to keep up the dog's energy in between meals, with plenty of water given. The dog needs time to settle down before and after any eating or drinking, so breaks should be factored into the training program or work routine.

EXERCISE

The Great Pyrenees is historically a guardian of sheep and, as such, tends to move at a leisurely pace. However, when they choose to be, Pyrenees can be quick and very agile. Exercise is necessary for both the health and happiness of

any dog, as well as for maintenance of a muscular condition. The exercise given depends very much on the home environment, but, if possible, a good walk each day, with plenty of opportunity for free run in a safe environment should become routine in adulthood. Please remember, though, that until puppies are a year old, lead work should be very limited, and they should not be allowed to climb up and down stairs or to jump down from high levels.

Pyrenees need plenty of area in which to exercise freely. Since they also need to be walked on lead, it is essential that the owner be able to control such a large dog. When allowing a dog to run free, safety is of utmost importance. For this reason, all possible escape routes should be thoroughly checked out before letting a dog off the lead, and of course one's garden also needs to be safely enclosed by sturdy high fencing, which should be checked at regular intervals. If one does not wish the dog to have free access to the very extremities of the garden, a good-sized outdoor run should be constructed. Great Pyrenees should never be chained up, unsupervised, outdoors.

When allowing a Pyrenees to have free run in a public area, it is important that he is not allowed to jump up on people.

This is such a large breed that an accident could happen, albeit unintentionally. For this reason, sensible training from puppyhood is essential.

Many Great Pyrenees enjoy swimming when given the opportunity, but of course this should only be permitted in a safe environment and under supervision. Some adult Pyrenees also go out hiking with their owners, a few even carrying their very own set of saddle bags!

For overweight dogs, dietary changes and activity will help the goal of weight loss. (Sound familiar?) While they should of course be encouraged to be active, remember not to overdo it, as the excess weight is already putting strain on his vital organs and bones. As for active and working dogs, some of them never seem to tire! They will enjoy time spent with their owners doing things together.

Regardless of your dog's condition and activity level, exercise offers benefits to all dogs and owners. Consider the fact that dogs who are kept active are more stimulated both physically and mentally, meaning that they are less likely to become bored and lapse into destructive behavior. Also consider the benefits of one-on-one time with your dog every day, continually strengthening the bond between the two of you.

No exercise compares to a vigorous run on the beach with a worthy chum. Despite the Great Pyrenees's great size, this is a very active breed that thrives on free running and excitement.

A LOT OF GROWING TO DO!

A giant-breed puppy's growth period is a delicate time during which he must receive proper nutrition and exercise to prevent developmental problems. With such a large dog, a lot can go wrong if owners are not careful. A diet moderate in protein, fat and calories, along with the highest quality vitamin and mineral content, is recommended by many experienced in giant breeds. The key is never to encourage rapid growth at any stage, but rather to feed for growth at a consistent, even pace. Some breeders feel that an adult-formula food is better for a growing giant-breed puppy, as it does not contain the high levels of protein and fat contained in traditional growth-formula foods. Your breeder will be an excellent source of advice about feeding your puppy; he also should give you tips about healthy exercise for the developing pup, as you never want to subject him to activity that causes stress and strain on his growing bones, joints and muscles.

Furthermore, exercising together will improve health and longevity for both of you. You both need exercise, and now you both have a workout partner and motivator!

GROOMING

COAT MAINTENANCE

General grooming of a Great Pyrenees's coat is a relatively simple, but necessary, procedure. Because this breed sheds large amounts of coat, grooming should become a very important regular routine that aids in conditioning the coat. Even owners who do not show their dogs should pay attention to the coat about three times each week, giving it a thorough brushing and combing; this should be done daily during a molt.

Each owner will have his own preferences for the best type of grooming equipment to use, so you would be wise to discuss this with your breeder when buying your puppy. There are now many excellent pet stores in most areas of the country, and of course the widest range of equipment can be found on sale at major shows.

A slicker brush is good for initially removing any debris from the coat, while a steel rake, slicker brush or wide-toothed comb will help to remove any loose hairs from the undercoat.

This will be a particularly important part of the grooming procedure when the coat is molting, at which time the coat will need attention every day. A brush with nylon bristles can then be used to go over the entire coat, finishing off by using the slicker brush again. Obviously, head hair should be dealt with gently, and a soft, natural bristle brush is good for this area.

BATHING

In general, dogs need to be bathed only a few times a year, possibly more often if your dog gets into something messy or if he starts to smell like a dog. Show dogs are usually bathed before every show, which could be as frequent as weekly, although this depends on the owner. Bathing too frequently can have negative effects on the skin and coat, removing natural oils and causing dryness.

If you give your dog his first bath when he is young, he will become accustomed to the process. Wrestling a dog into the tub or chasing a freshly shampooed dog who has escaped from the bath will be no fun! Most dogs don't naturally enjoy their baths, but you at least want them to cooperate with you.

Before bathing the dog, have the items you'll need close at hand. First, decide where you will bathe the dog. You should have a tub or basin with a non-slip

---

PUPPY LE PEW

On that ill-fated day when your puppy insults the neighborhood skunk by calling him a weasel, you will likely have the unhappy chore of "de-skunking" your dog. Skunks are not afraid of dogs (no less puppies) and will take on an approaching "predator." The skunk's spray is a nasty compound called thiols, a thick, oily liquid that can also be found in decaying flesh or feces. After the skunk hisses, growls and does his "don't-mess-with-me" dance, he sprays the unsuspecting canine.

The age-old remedy was to bathe a "skunked" dog in tomato juice, but thanks to chemist Paul Krebaum, you can put away your can opener. Krebaum provides us with this easy and effective recipe to deodorize your stinky puppy: 1 quart 3% hydrogen peroxide; ¼ cup baking soda; and 1 teaspoon liquid dish detergent. Work the soapy formula into the dog's coat and keep it out of the dog's eyes. Rinse the dog thoroughly after the bath. Do not make this formula and attempt to bottle it—it will explode! Incidentally, the skunk is in fact a weasel, but there's no sense arguing with the nasty-tempered mouse-eating fellow.

---

surface. Puppies can even be bathed in a sink. In warm weather, some like to use a portable pool in the yard, although you'll want to make sure your dog doesn't head for the

Selecting the Right Brushes and Combs

Will a rubber curry make my dog look slicker? Is a rake smaller than a pin brush? Do I choose nylon or natural bristles? Buying a dog brush can make the hairs on your head stand on end! Here's a quick once-over to educate you on the different types of brushes.

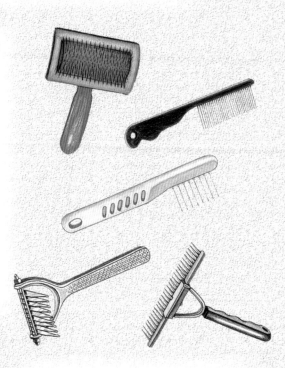

Slicker Brush: Fine metal prongs closely set on a curved base. Used to remove dead coat from the undercoat of medium- to long-coated breeds.

Pin Brush: Metal pins, often covered with rubber tips, set on an oval base. Used to remove shedding hair and is gentler than a slicker brush.

Metal Comb: Steel teeth attached to a steel handle; the closeness and size of the teeth vary greatly. A "flea comb" has tiny teeth set very closely together and is used to find fleas in a dog's coat. Combs with wider teeth are used for detangling longer coats.

Rake: Long-toothed comb with a short handle. Used to remove undercoat from heavily coated breeds with dense undercoats.

Soft-bristle Brush: Nylon or natural bristles set in a plastic or wood base. Used on short coats or long coats (without undercoats).

Rubber Curry: Rubber prongs, with or without a handle. Used for short-coated dogs. Good for use during shampooing.

Combination Brushes: Two-sided brush with a different type of bristle on each side; for example, pin brush on one side and slicker on the other, or bristle brush on one side and pin brush on the other. An economic choice if you need two kinds of brushes.

Grooming Glove: Sometimes called a hound glove, used to give sleek-coated dogs a once-over.

nearest dirt pile following his bath! You will also need a hose or shower spray to wet the coat thoroughly, a shampoo formulated for dogs, absorbent towels and perhaps a blow dryer. Human shampoos are too harsh for dogs' coats and will dry them out.

Before wetting the dog, give him a brush-through to remove any dead hair, dirt and mats. Make sure he is at ease in the tub and have the water at a comfortable temperature. Begin bathing by wetting the coat all the way down to the skin. Massage in the shampoo, keeping it away from his face and eyes. Rinse him thoroughly, again avoiding the eyes and ears, as you don't want to get water in the ear canals. A thorough rinsing is important, as shampoo residue is drying and itchy to the dog. After rinsing, wrap him in a towel to absorb the initial moisture. You can finish drying with either a towel or a blow dryer on low heat, held at a safe distance from the dog. You should keep the dog indoors and away from drafts until he is completely dry.

NAIL CLIPPING

Having his nails trimmed is not on many dogs' lists of favorite things to do. With this in mind, you will need to accustom your puppy to the procedure at a young age so that he will sit still (well, as still as he can) for his

The puppy should welcome the feeling of a soft nylon brush on its coat.

Acclimated to grooming by its breeder, your puppy will hopefully be the handsome model of patience and glamor that this puppy is.

Keep grooming sessions short and sweet lest your Pyrenees lose heart.

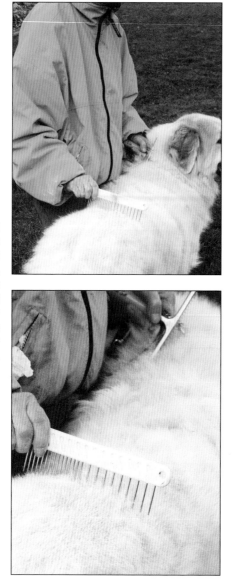

A wide-toothed comb, applied to the undercoat during shedding, will limit the amount of Pyrenees hair that floats around your home.

ally scratch, not good for you!

Some dogs' nails are worn down naturally by regular walking on hard surfaces, so the frequency with which you clip depends on your individual dog. Look at his nails from time to time and clip as needed; a good way to know when it's time for a trim is if you hear your dog clicking as he walks across the floor.

There are several types of nail clippers and even electric nail-grinding tools made for dogs; first we'll discuss using the clipper. To start, have your clipper ready and pedicures. Long nails can cause the dog's feet to spread, which is not good for him; likewise, long nails can hurt if they unintention-

---

WATER SHORTAGE

No matter how well-behaved your dog is, bathing is always a project! Nothing can substitute for a good warm bath, but owners do have the option of giving their dogs "dry" baths. Pet shops sell excellent products, in both powder and spray forms, designed for spot-cleaning your dog. These dry shampoos are convenient for touch-up jobs when you don't have the time to bathe your dog in the traditional way.

Muddy feet, messy behinds and smelly coats can be spot-cleaned and deodorized with a "wet-nap"-style cleaner. On those days when your dog insists on rolling in fresh goose droppings and there's no time for a bath, a spot bath can save the day. These pre-moistened wipes are also handy for other grooming needs like wiping faces, ears and eyes and freshening tails and behinds.

some doggie treats on hand. You want your pup to view his nail-clipping sessions in a positive light, and what better way to convince him than with food? You may want to enlist the help of an assistant to comfort the pup and offer treats as you concentrate on the clipping itself. The guillotine-type clipper is thought of by many as the easiest type to use; the nail tip is inserted into the opening and blades on the top and bottom snip it off in one clip.

Start by grasping the pup's paw; a little pressure on the foot pad causes the nail to extend, making it easier to clip. Clip off a little at a time. If you can see the "quick," which is a blood vessel that runs through each nail, you will know how much to trim, as you do not want to cut into the quick. On that note, if you do cut the quick, which will cause bleeding, you can stem the flow of blood with a styptic pencil or other clotting agent. If you mistakenly nip the quick, do not panic or fuss, as this will cause the pup to be afraid. Simply reassure the pup, stop the bleeding and move on to the next nail. Don't be discouraged; you will become a professional canine pedicurist with practice!

You may or may not be able to see the quick, so it's best to just clip off a small bit at a time. If you see a dark dot in the center of the nail, this is the quick and your

The slicker brush is ideal for removing debris from the Great Pyrenees's thick coat.

Use a brush with nylon bristles to help remove loose hairs, especially during the shedding season.

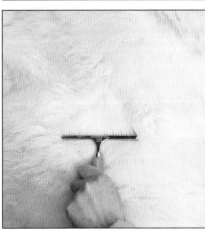

The grooming rake helps to manage the undercoat.

cue to stop clipping. Tell the puppy he's a "good boy" and offer a piece of treat with each nail. You can also use nail-clipping time to examine the footpads, making sure that they are not dry and cracked and that nothing has become embedded in them.

The nail grinder, the second choice, is many owners' first choice. Accustoming the puppy to the sound of the grinder and sensation of the buzz presents fewer challenges than the clipper, and there's no chance of cutting through the quick. Use the grinder on a low setting and always talk soothingly to your dog. He won't mind his salon visit, and he'll have nicely polished nails as well.

EAR CLEANING

While keeping your dog's ears clean unfortunately will not cause him to "hear" your commands any better, it will protect him from ear infection and ear mite infestation. In addition, a dog's ears are vulnerable to waxy build-up and to collecting foreign matter from the outdoors. Look in your dog's ears regularly to ensure that they look pink, clean and otherwise healthy. Even if they look fine, an odor in the ears signals a problem and means it's time to call the vet.

A dog's ears should be cleaned regularly; once a week is suggested, and you can do this along with your regular brushing.

Using a cotton ball or pad, and never probing into the ear canal, wipe the ear gently. You can use an ear-cleansing liquid or powder available from your vet or pet-supply store, or some owners prefer to use home-made solutions with ingredients like one-part white vinegar and one-part hydrogen peroxide. Ask your vet about home remedies before you attempt to concoct something on your own!

Keep your dog's ears free of excess hair by plucking it as needed. If done gently, this will be painless for the dog. Look for wax, brown droppings (a sign of ear mites), redness or any other abnormalities. At the first sign of a problem, contact your vet so that he can prescribe an appropriate medication.

EYE CARE

During grooming sessions, pay extra attention to the condition of your dog's eyes. If the area around

---

CLIPPING THE QUICK

If your Great Pyrenees tears its nail, nail polish (of the most simple kind, of course) is a quick sealant. This helps stem the flow of blood and acts as a preventative against getting dirt into the wound. It is important to keep the foot dry and as clean as possible. The homeopathic puncture wound remedy Hypericum 1M/Ledum 200c is also worth a try.

the eyes is soiled or if tear staining has occurred, there are various cleaning agents made especially for this purpose. Look at the dog's eyes to make sure no debris has entered; dogs with large eyes and those who spend time outdoors are especially prone to this.

The signs of an eye infection are obvious: mucus, redness, puffiness, scabs or other signs of irritation. If your dog's eyes become infected, the vet will likely prescribe an antibiotic ointment for treatment. If you notice signs of more serious problems, such as opacities in the eye, which usually indicate cataracts, consult the vet at once. Taking time to pay attention to your dog's eyes will alert you in the early stages of any problem so that you can get your dog treatment as soon as possible. You could save your dog's sight!

A Clean Smile

Another essential part of grooming is brushing your dog's teeth and checking his overall oral condition. Studies show that around 80% of dogs experience dental problems by two years of age, and the percentage is higher in older dogs. Therefore, it is highly likely that your dog will have trouble with his teeth and gums unless you are proactive with home dental care.

The most common dental

Tear stains can be removed with special cleansers available from your veterinarian or pet shop.

Your dog's ears should be cleaned on a regular basis with an ear-cleaning solution and a soft cotton wipe.

Keep an eye on your pup's growing teeth. Report any abnormalities to your vet.

problem in dogs is plaque build-up. If not treated, this causes gum disease, infection and resultant tooth loss. Bacteria from these infections spread throughout the body, affecting the vital organs. Do you need much more convincing to start brushing your dog's teeth? If so, take a good whiff of your dog's breath, and read on.

Fortunately, home dental care is rather easy and convenient for pet owners. Specially formulated canine toothpaste is easy to find. You should use one of these, not a product for humans. Some doggie pastes are even available in flavors appealing to dogs. If your dog likes the flavor, he will tolerate the process better, making things much easier for you! Doggie toothbrushes come in different sizes and are designed to

Keep your Pyr's choppers in top form by brushing regularly and visiting the vet.

SCOOTING HIS BOTTOM

Here's a doggy problem that many owners tend to neglect. If your dog is scooting his rear end around the carpet, he probably is experiencing anal-sac impaction or blockage. The anal sacs are the two grape-sized glands on either side of the dog's vent. The dog cannot empty these glands, which become filled with a foul-smelling material. The dog may attempt to lick the area to relieve the pressure. He may also rub his anus on your walls, furniture or floors.

Don't neglect your dog's rear end during grooming sessions. By squeezing both sides of the anus with a soft cloth, you can express some of the material in the sacs. If the material is pasty and thick, you likely will need the assistance of a veterinarian. Vets know how to express the glands and can show you how to do it correctly without hurting the dog or spraying yourself with poop.

fit the contour of a canine mouth. Rubber fingertip brushes fit right on one of your fingers and have rubber nodes to clean the teeth and massage the gums. This may be easier to handle, as it is akin to rubbing your dog's teeth with your finger.

As with all grooming tasks, accustom your pup to his dental care early on. Start gently, for a few minutes at a time, so that he gets used to the feel of the brush and to your handling his mouth. Offer praise and petting so that he looks at tooth-care time as a time when he gets extra love and attention. The routine should become second nature; at the very least, he should at least tolerate it.

Aside from brushing, offer dental toys to your dog and feed crunchy biscuits, which help to minimize plaque. Rope toys have the added benefit of acting like floss as the dog chews. At your adult dog's yearly check-ups, the vet will likely perform a thorough tooth scraping as well as a complete check for any problems. Proper care of your dog's teeth will ensure that you will enjoy your dog's smile for many years to come. The next time your dog goes to give you a hello kiss, you'll be glad you spent the time caring for his teeth.

THE OTHER END

Dogs sometime have troubles with their anal glands, which are sacs located beside the anal vent. These should empty when a dog has normal bowel movements but, if not, they can become full or impacted, causing discomfort for a dog. Owners often are alarmed to see their dogs' scooting across the floor, dragging their behinds behind! This is a dog's attempt to empty the glands himself.

Some brave owners attempt to evacuate their dogs' anal glands themselves during grooming, but

Acclimate your puppy to traveling in the car, though it's not necessary to give up the front seat. If possible, use your pup's crate for travel, otherwise invest in a harness or safety gate.

no one will tell you that this is a pleasant task! Thus, many owners prefer to make the trip to the vet to have the vet take care of the problem; others whose dogs visit a groomer can have this done by the groomer if he offers this as part of his services. Regardless, don't neglect the dog's other end in your home-care routine and look for scooting, licking or other signs of discomfort "back there" to ascertain if the anal glands need to be emptied.

BASIC TRAINING PRINCIPLES: PUPPY VS. ADULT

There's a big difference between training an adult dog and training a young puppy. With a young puppy, everything is new! At eight to ten weeks of age, he will be experiencing many things, and he has nothing to which to compare these experiences. Up to this point, he has been wth his dam and littermates, not one-on-one with people except in his interactions with his breeder and visitors to the litter.

When you first bring the puppy home, he is eager to please you. This means that he accepts doing things your way! During the next couple of months, he will absorb the basis of everything he needs to know for the rest of his life. This early age is even referred to as the "sponge" stage. After that, for the next 18 months, it's up to you to reinforce good manners by building on the foundation that you've established. Once your puppy is

Facing page: Pyrenees are interactive, super-intelligent dogs that respond to considerate training methods. Never treat a Great Pyrenees harshly.

THE RIGHT START

The best advice for a potential dog owner is to start with the very best puppy that money can buy. Don't shop around for a bargain in the newspaper. You're buying a companion, not a used Buick or a second-hand Maytag. The purchase price of the dog represents the most important part of the investment, but this is indeed a very small sum compared to the expenses of maintaining the dog in good health. If you purchase a well-bred, healthy and sound puppy, you will be starting right. An unhealthy puppy can cost you thousands of dollars in unnecessary veterinary expenses and, possibly, a fortune in heartbreak as well.

Positive reinforcement is the basis of most training strategies. Keep your puppy's attention and encourage him for every good thing, and you will have an amenable, enthusiastic Great Pyrenees.

OUR CANINE KIDS

"Everything I learned about parenting, I learned from my dog." How often adults recognize that their parenting skills are mere extensions of the education they acquired while caring for their dogs! Many owners refer to their dogs as their "kids" and treat their canine companions like real members of the family. Surveys indicate that a majority of dog owners talk to their dogs regularly, celebrate their dogs' birthdays and purchase Christmas gifts for their dogs. Another survey shows that dog owners take their dogs to the veterinarian more frequently than they visit their own physicians.

of the interesting sports, games and activities available to pet owners and their dogs.

Raising your puppy is a family affair. Each member of the family must know what rules to set forth for the puppy and how to use the same one-word commands to mean exactly the same thing every time. Even if yours is a large family, one person will soon be considered by the pup to be the leader, the Alpha person in his pack, the "boss" who must be obeyed. Often that highly regarded person turns out to be the one who feeds the puppy. Food ranks very high on the puppy's list of important things! That's why your puppy is rewarded with small treats along with verbal praise when he responds to you correctly. As the puppy learns to do what you want him to do, the food rewards are gradually eliminated and only the praise remains. If you keep up with the food treats, you could have two problems on your hands—an obese dog and a beggar.

Training begins the minute your puppy steps through the doorway of your home, so don't make the mistake of putting the puppy on the floor and telling him by your actions, "Go for it! Run wild!" Even if this is your first puppy, you must act as if you know what you're doing: be the boss. An uncertain pup may be

reliable in basic commands and behavior, and has reached the appropriate age, you may gradually introduce him to some

BASIC PRINCIPLES OF DOG TRAINING

1. Start training early. A young puppy is ready, willing and able.
2. Timing is your all-important tool. Praise at the exact time that the dog responds correctly. Pay close attention.
3. Patience is almost as important as timing!
4. Repeat! The same word has to mean the same thing every time. Puppies often play the "Oh, I forgot!" game.
5. In the beginning, praise all correct behavior verbally, along with treats and petting.

terrified to move, while a bold one will be ready to take you at your word and start plotting to destroy the house! Before you collected your puppy, you decided where his own special place would be, and that's where to put him when you first arrive home. Give him a house tour after he has investigated his area, had a nap and a bathroom "pit stop."

It's worth mentioning here that if you've adopted an adult dog that is completely trained to your liking, lucky you! You're off the hook! However, if that dog spent his life up to this point in a kennel, or even in a good home but without any real training, be prepared to tackle the job ahead. A dog three years of age or older with no previous training cannot be blamed for not knowing what he was never taught. While the dog is trying to understand and learn your rules, at the same time he has to unlearn many of his previously self-taught habits and general view of the world.

Working with a professional trainer will speed up your progress with an adopted adult dog. You'll need patience, too. Some new rules may be close to impossible for the dog to accept. After all, he's been successful so far by doing everything his way! (Patience again.) He may agree with your instruction for a few days and then slip back into his old ways, so you must be just as consistent and understanding in your teaching as you would be with a puppy. (More patience needed yet again!) Your dog has to learn to pay attention to your voice, your family, the daily routine, new smells, new sounds

A six-week-old Great Pyrenees puppy will be glued to your every word, though a little tasty tidbit doesn't hurt either!

and, in some cases, even a new climate.

One of the most important things to find out about a newly adopted adult dog is his reaction to children (yours and others), strangers and your friends, and how he acts upon meeting other dogs. If he was not socialized with dogs as a puppy, this could be a major problem. This does not mean that he's a "bad" dog, a vicious dog or an aggressive dog; rather, it means that he has no idea how to read another dog's body language. There's no way for him to tell if the other dog is a friend or foe. Survival instinct

Lead training and house-training go hand in hand. You can practice lead training on the way to the pup's outdoor relief area.

> ### SOMEBODY TO BLAME
> House-training a puppy can be frustrating for the puppy and the owner alike. The puppy does not instinctively understand the difference between defecating on the pavement outside and piddling on the ceramic tile in the kitchen. He is confused and frightened by his human's exuberant reactions to his natural urges. The owner, arguably the more intelligent of the duo, is also frustrated that he cannot convince his puppy to obey his commands and instructions.
>
> In frustration, the owner may struggle with the temptation to discipline the puppy, scold him or even strike the puppy on the rear end. Shouting and smacking the puppy may make you feel better, but it will defeat your purpose in gaining your puppy's trust and respect. Don't blame your nine-week-old puppy. Blame yourself for not being 100% consistent in the puppy's lessons and routine. The lesson here is simple: try harder and your puppy will succeed, too.

takes over, telling him to attack first and ask questions later. This definitely calls for professional help and, even then, may not be a behavior that can be corrected 100% reliably (or even at all). If you have a puppy, this is why it is so very important to introduce your young puppy properly to other puppies and "dog-friendly" adult dogs.

House-training revolves around predicting where the puppy will piddle! You must attach more than a little importance to your puppy's needs!

HOUSE-TRAINING

Dogs are tactile-oriented when it comes to house-training. In other words, they respond to the surface on which they are given approval to eliminate. The choice is yours (the dog's version is in parentheses): The lawn (including the neighbors' lawns)? A bare patch of earth under a tree (where people like to sit and relax in the summertime)? Concrete steps or patio (all sidewalks, garage and basement floors)? The curbside (watch out for cars)? A small area of crushed stone in a corner of the yard (mine!)? The latter is the best choice if you can manage it, because it will remain strictly for the dog's use and is easy to keep clean.

You can start out with paper-training indoors and switch over to an outdoor surface as the puppy matures and gains control over his need to eliminate. For the nay-sayers, don't worry—this won't mean that the dog will soil on every piece of newspaper lying around the house. You are training him to go outside, remember? Starting out by paper-training often is the only choice for a city dog.

WHEN YOUR PUPPY'S "GOT TO GO"
Your puppy's need to relieve himself is seemingly non-stop, but signs of improvement will be seen each week. From 8 to 10 weeks old, the puppy will have to be taken outside every time he wakes up, about 10-15 minutes after every meal and after every period

of play—all day long, from first thing in the morning until his bedtime! That's a total of ten or more trips per day to teach the puppy where it's okay to relieve himself. With that schedule in mind, you can see that house-training a young puppy is not a part-time job. It requires someone to be home all day.

KIDS RULE

Children of 10 to 12 year of age are old enough to understand the "be kind to dumb animals" approach and will have fun training their dogs, especially to do tricks. It teaches them to be tolerant, patient and appreciative as well as to accept failure to some extent. Children of four, five or six years of age can be tyrants, making unreasonable demands of the dog and unable to cope with defeat, blaming it all on the dog. Toddlers need not apply.

If that seems overwhelming or impossible, do a little planning. For example, plan to pick up your puppy at the start of a vacation period. If you can't get home in the middle of the day, plan to hire a dog-sitter or ask a neighbor to come over to take the pup outside, feed him his lunch and then take him out again about ten or so minutes after he's eaten. Also make arrangements with that person or another to be your "emergency" contact if you have to stay late on the job. Remind yourself—repeatedly—that this hectic schedule improves as the puppy gets older.

HOME WITHIN A HOME

Your puppy needs to be confined to one secure puppy-proof area when no one is able to watch his every move. Generally, the kitchen is the place of choice because the floor is washable. Likewise, it's a busy family area that will accustom the pup to a variety of noises, everything from pots and pans to the telephone, blender and dishwasher. He will also be enchanted by the smell of your cooking (and will never be critical when you burn something). An exercise pen (also called an "ex-pen," a puppy version of a playpen) within the room of choice is an excellent means of confinement for a young pup. He can see out and has a certain amount of space in which

CANINE DEVELOPMENT SCHEDULE

It is important to understand how and at what age a puppy develops into adulthood. If you are a puppy owner, consult the following Canine Development Schedule to determine the stage of development your puppy is currently experiencing. This knowledge will help you as you work with the puppy in the weeks and months ahead.

PERIOD	AGE	CHARACTERISTICS
FIRST TO THIRD	BIRTH TO SEVEN WEEKS	Puppy needs food, sleep and warmth and responds to simple and gentle touching. Needs mother for security and disciplining. Needs littermates for learning and interacting with other dogs. Pup learns to function within a pack and learns pack order of dominance. Begin socializing pup with adults and children for short periods. Pup begins to become aware of his environment.
FOURTH	EIGHT TO TWELVE WEEKS	Brain is fully developed. Pup needs socializing with outside world. Remove from mother and littermates. Needs to change from canine pack to human pack. Human dominance necessary. Fear period occurs between 8 and 12 weeks. Avoid fright and pain.
FIFTH	THIRTEEN TO SIXTEEN WEEKS	Training and formal obedience should begin. Less association with other dogs, more with people, places, situations. Period will pass easily if you remember this is pup's change-to-adolescence time. Be firm and fair. Flight instinct prominent. Permissiveness and over-disciplining can do permanent damage. Praise for good behavior.
JUVENILE	FOUR TO EIGHT MONTHS	Another fear period about 7 to 8 months of age. It passes quickly, but be cautious of fright and pain. Sexual maturity reached. Dominant traits established. Dog should understand sit, down, come and stay by now.

NOTE: THESE ARE APPROXIMATE TIME FRAMES. ALLOW FOR INDIVIDUAL DIFFERENCES IN PUPPIES.

Walking the puppy naturally stimulates the dog to want to relieve himself. Don't be too impatient when he wants to stop, rest or sniff.

Crates are something that pet owners are at last getting used to for their dogs. Wild or domestic canines have always preferred to sleep in den-like safe spots, and that is exactly what the crate provides. How often have you seen adult dogs that choose to sleep under a table or chair even though they have full run of the house? It's the den connection.

The crate should be big enough for the adult dog to stand up and turn around in, even though he may spend much of his

to run about, but he is safe from dangerous things like electrical cords, heating units, trash baskets or open kitchen-supply cabinets. Place the pen where the puppy will not get a blast of heat or air conditioning.

In the pen, you can put a few toys, his bed (which can be his crate if the dimensions of pen and crate are compatible) and a few layers of newspaper in one small corner, just in case. A water bowl can be hung at a convenient height on the side of the ex-pen so it won't become a splashing pool for an innovative puppy. His food dish can go on the floor, next to the water bowl.

LEASH TRAINING

House-training and leash training go hand in hand, literally. When taking your puppy outside to do his business, lead him there on his leash. Unless an emergency potty run is called for, do not whisk the puppy in your arms and take him outside. If you have a fenced yard, you have the advantage of letting the puppy loose to go out, but it's better to put the dog on the leash and take him to his designated place in the yard until he is reliably house-trained. Taking the puppy for a walk is the best way to house-train a dog. The dog will associate the walk with his time to relieve himself and the exercise of walking stimulates the dog's bowels and bladder. Dogs that are not trained to relieve themselves on a walk may hold it until they get back home, which of course defeats half the purpose of the walk.

time curled up in the back part of it. There are movable barriers that fit inside dog crates to provide the right amount of space for small puppies that grow into large dogs. Never afford a young puppy too much space, thinking that you're being kind and generous. He'll just sleep at one end of the crate and soil in the other end! While you should purchase only one crate, one that will accommodate your pup when grown, you will need to make use of the partitions so that the pup has a comfortable area without enough extra space to use as a toilet. A dog does not like to soil where he sleeps, so you are teaching him to "hold it" until it's time for a trip outside. You may want an extra crate to keep in the car for safe traveling.

In your "happy" voice, use the word "Crate" every time you put the pup in his den. If he's new to a crate, toss in a small biscuit for him to chase the first few times. At night, after he's been outside, he should sleep in his crate. The crate may be kept in his designated area at night or, if you want to be sure to hear those wake-up yips in the morning, put the crate in a corner of your bedroom. However, don't make any response whatsoever to whining or crying. If he's completely ignored, he'll settle down and get to sleep.

Good bedding for a young puppy is an old folded bath towel

POTTY COMMAND

Most dogs love to please their masters, and there are no bounds to what dogs will do to make their owners happy. The potty command is a good example of this theory. If toileting on command makes the master happy, then more power to him. Puppies will obligingly piddle if it really makes their keepers smile. Some owners can be creative about which word they will use to command their dogs to relieve themselves. Some popular choices are "Potty," "Tinkle," "Piddle," "Let's go," "Hurry up" and "Toilet." Give the command every time your puppy goes into position and the puppy will begin to associate his business with the command.

or an old blanket, something that is easily washable and disposable if necessary ("accidents" will happen!). Never put newspaper into the puppy's crate. Those old ideas of adding a clock to replace his mother's heartbeat, or a hot-water bottle to replace her warmth, are just that—old ideas. The clock could drive the puppy nuts, and the hot-water bottle could end up as a very soggy waterbed! An extremely good breeder would have introduced

EXTRA! EXTRA!

The headlines read: "Puppy Piddles Here!" Breeders commonly use newspapers to line their whelping pens, so puppies learn to associate newspapers with relieving themselves. Do not use newspapers to line your pup's crate, as this will signal to your puppy that it is OK to urinate in his crate. If you choose to paper-train your puppy, you will layer newspapers on a section of the floor near the door he uses to go outside. You should encourage the puppy to use the papers to relieve himself, and bring him there whenever you see him getting ready to go. Little by little, you will reduce the size of the newspaper-covered area so that the puppy will learn to relieve himself "on the other side of the door."

your puppy to the crate by letting two pups sleep together for a couple of nights, followed by several nights alone. How thankful you will be if you found that breeder!

Safe toys in the pup's crate or area will keep him occupied, but monitor their condition closely. Discard any toys that show signs of being chewed to bits. Squeaky parts, bits of stuffing or plastic or any other small pieces can cause intestinal blockage or possibly choking if swallowed.

PROGRESSING WITH POTTY-TRAINING
After you've taken your puppy out and he has relieved himself in the area you've selected, he can have some free time with the family as long as there is someone responsible for watching him. That doesn't mean just someone in the same room who is watching TV or busy on the computer, but one person who is doing nothing other than keeping an eye on the pup, playing with him on the floor and helping him understand his position in the pack.

This first taste of freedom will let you begin to set the house rules. If you don't want the dog on the furniture, now is the time to prevent his first attempts to jump up onto the couch. The word to use in this case is "Off," not "Down." "Down" is the word you will use to teach the down position, which is something entirely different.

Most corrections at this stage come in the form of simply distracting the puppy. Instead of telling him "No" for "Don't chew the carpet," distract the chomping puppy with a toy and he'll forget about the carpet.

As you are playing with the pup, do not forget to watch him closely and pay attention to his body language. Whenever you see him begin to circle or sniff, take the puppy outside to relieve himself. If you are paper-training, put him back in his confined area on the newspapers. In either case, praise him as he eliminates, while he actually is in the act of relieving himself. Three seconds after he has finished is too late! You'll be praising him for running toward you, or picking up a toy or whatever he may be doing at that moment, and that's not what you want to be praising him for. Timing is a vital tool in all dog training. Use it!

Remove soiled newspapers immediately and replace them with clean ones. You may want to take a small piece of soiled paper and place it in the middle of the new clean papers, as the scent will attract him to that spot when it's time to go again. That scent attraction is why it's so important to clean up any messes made in the house with a product specially made to eliminate the

odor of dog urine and droppings. Regular household cleansers won't do the trick. Pet shops sell the best pet deodorizers. Invest in the largest container you can find.

Scent attraction eventually will lead your pup to his chosen spot outdoors; this is the basis of outdoor training. When you take your puppy outside to relieve himself, use a one-word command such as "Outside" or "Go-potty" (that's one word to the puppy!) as you pick him up and attach his leash. Then put him down in his area. If he is too big for you to carry, snap the leash on quickly and lead him to his spot. Now comes the hard part—hard for you, that is. Just stand there until he urinates and defecates. Move

Quiet socialization time with the family children will nurture the bond between the Great Pyrenees puppy and his people.

him a few feet in one direction or another if he's just sitting there, looking at you, but remember that this is neither playtime nor time for a walk. This is strictly a business trip! Then, as he circles and squats (remember your timing!), give him a quiet "Good dog" as praise. If you start to jump for joy, ecstatic over his performance, he'll do one of two things: either he will stop mid-stream, as it were, or he'll do it again for

When training your Pyr puppy, don't overdo the treats. A handful of goodies can equal half a meal and offset the puppy's balanced diet.

I WILL FOLLOW YOU
Obedience isn't just a classroom activity. In your home, you have many great opportunities to teach your dog polite manners. Allowing your pet on the bed or furniture elevates him to your level, which is not a good idea (the word is "Off!"). Use the "umbilical cord" method, keeping your dog on lead so he has to go with you wherever you go. You sit, he sits. You walk, he heels. You stop, he sit-stays. Everywhere you go, he's with you, but you go first!

you—in the house—and expect you to be just as delighted!

Give him five minutes or so and, if he doesn't go in that time, take him back indoors to his confined area and try again in another ten minutes, or immediately if you see him sniffing and circling. By careful observation, you'll soon work out a successful schedule.

Accidents, by the way, are just that—accidents. Clean them up quickly and thoroughly, without comment, after the puppy has been taken outside to finish his business and then put back in his area or crate. If you witness an accident in progress, say "No!" in a stern voice and get the pup outdoors immediately. No punishment is needed. You and your puppy are just learning each other's language and sometimes it's easy to miss a puppy's message. Chalk it up to experience and watch more closely from now on.

KEEPING THE PACK ORDERLY
Discipline is a form of training that brings order to life. For example, military discipline is what allows the soldiers in an army to work as one. Discipline is a form of teaching and, in dogs, is the basis of how the successful pack operates. Each member knows his place in the pack and all respect the leader, or Alpha dog. It is essential for your puppy that you establish this type of relationship, with you as the Alpha, or leader. It is a form of social coexistence that all canines recognize and accept. Discipline, therefore, is never to be confused with punishment. When you teach your puppy how you want him to behave, and he behaves properly and you praise him for

it, you are disciplining him with a form of positive reinforcement.

For a dog, rewards come in the form of praise, a smile, a cheerful tone of voice, a few friendly pats or a rub of the ears. Rewards are also small food treats. Obviously, that does not mean bits of regular dog food. Rather, treats are very small bits of special things like cheese or pieces of soft dog treats. The idea is to reward the dog with something very small that he can taste and swallow, providing instant positive reinforcement. If he has to take time to chew the treat, by the time he is finished he will have forgotten what he did to earn it!

Your puppy should never be physically punished. The displeasure shown on your face and in your voice is sufficient to signal to the pup that he has done

Breeders spend time interacting with, handling and teaching good manners to the baby puppies so that they will be well adjusted and amenable to training in their new homes.

"SCHOOL" MODE
When is your puppy ready for a lesson? Maybe not always when you are. Attempting training with treats just before his mealtime is asking for disaster. Notice what times of day he performs best and make that Fido's school time.

something wrong. He wants to please everyone higher up on the social ladder, especially his leader, so a scowl and harsh voice will take care of the error. Growling out the word "Shame!" when the pup is caught in the act of doing something wrong is better than the repetitive "No." Some dogs hear "No" so often that they begin to think it's their name! By the way, do not use the dog's name when you're correcting him. His name is reserved to get his attention for something pleasant about to take place.

There are punishments that have nothing to do with you. For example, your dog may think that chasing cats is one reason for his existence. You can try to stop it as much as you like without success because it's such fun for the dog. But one good hissing, spitting, swipe of a cat's claws across the dog's nose will put an end to the game forever. Only intervene when your dog's eyeball is seriously at risk. Cat scratches can cause permanent damage to an innocent but annoying puppy.

PUPPY KINDERGARTEN

Collar and Leash
Before you begin your puppy's education, he must be used to his collar and leash. Choose a collar for your puppy that is secure, but not heavy or bulky. He won't enjoy training if he's uncomfort-

> **BOOT CAMP**
> Even if one member of the family assumes the role of "drill sergeant," every member of the family has to know what's involved in the dog's education. Success depends on consistency and knowing what words to use, how to use them, how to say them and, most important to the dog, how to praise. The dog will be happy to respond to all members of the family, but don't make the little guy think he's in boot camp!

able. A flat buckle collar is fine for everyday wear and for initial puppy training. For older dogs, there are several types of training collars such as the martingale, which is a double loop that tightens slightly around the neck, or the head collar, which is similar to a horse's halter. Do not use a chain choke collar unless you have been specifically shown how to put it on and how to use it. Coated breeds like Great Pyrenees are not suited to chain chokes.

A lightweight 6-foot woven cotton or nylon training leash is preferred by most trainers because it is easy to fold up in your hand and comfortable to hold because there is a certain amount of give to it. There are lessons where the dog will start off six feet away from you at the end of the leash. The leash used to take the puppy outside to relieve himself is shorter because you don't want him to roam away from his area. The shorter leash will also be the one to use when you walk the puppy for the same reason.

If you've been fortunate enough to enroll in a Puppy Kindergarten Training class, suggestions will be made as to the best collar and leash for your young puppy. I say "fortunate" because your puppy will be in a class with puppies in his age range (up to five months old) of all breeds and sizes. It's the perfect way for him to learn the right way (and the wrong way) to interact with other dogs as well as their people. You cannot teach your puppy how to interpret another dog's sign language. For a first-time puppy owner, these socialization classes are invaluable. For experienced dog owners, they are a real boon to further training.

ATTENTION
You've been using the dog's name since the minute you collected him from the breeder, so you should be able to get his attention by saying his name—with a big smile and in an excited tone of voice. His response will be the puppy equivalent of "Here I am! What are we going to do?" Your

immediate response (if you haven't guessed by now) is "Good dog." Rewarding him at the moment he pays attention to you teaches him the proper way to respond when he hears his name.

EXERCISES FOR A BASIC CANINE EDUCATION

THE SIT EXERCISE
There are several ways to teach the puppy to sit. The first one is to catch him whenever he is about to sit and, as his backside nears the floor, say "Sit, good dog!"

Training a dog to sit requires both verbal communication (teaching the dog to recognize the sound of the word "sit") as well as physical contact so that the dog understands what is expected of him.

That's positive reinforcement and, if your timing is sharp, he will learn that what he's doing at that second is connected to your saying "Sit" and that you think he's clever for doing it!

Another method is to start with the puppy on his leash in front of you. Show him a treat in the palm of your right hand. Bring your hand up under his nose and, almost in slow motion, move your hand up and back so his nose goes up in the air and his head tilts back as he follows the treat in your hand. At that point, he will have to either sit or fall over, so as his back legs buckle under, say "Sit, good dog," and then give

Food and praise are keys to teaching the Great Pyrenees puppy to sit/stay. Be patient and positive and your pup will respond in due course.

him the treat and lots of praise. You may have to begin with your hand lightly running up his chest, actually lifting his chin up until he sits. Some (usually older) Great Pyrenees require gentle pressure on their hindquarters with the left hand, in which case the dog should be on your left side. Puppies generally do not appreciate this physical dominance.

After a few times, you should be able to show the dog a treat in the open palm of your hand, raise your hand waist high as you say "Sit" and have him sit. Once again, you have taught him two things at the same time. The verbal command and the motion of the hand are both signals for the sit. Your puppy is watching you almost more than he is listening to you, so what you do is

just as important as what you say.

Don't save any of these drills only for training sessions. Use them as much as possible at odd times during a normal day. The dog should always sit before being given his food dish. He should sit to let you go through a doorway first, when the doorbell rings or when you stop to speak to someone on the street.

THE DOWN EXERCISE

Before beginning to teach the down command, you must consider how the dog feels about this exercise. To him, "down" is a submissive position. Being flat on the floor with you standing over him is not his idea of fun. It's up to you to let him know that, while it may not be fun, the reward of your approval is worth his effort.

Start with the puppy on your left side in a sit position. Hold the

---

DOWN

"Down" is a harsh-sounding word and a submissive posture in dog body language, thus presenting two obstacles in teaching the down command. When the dog is about to flop down on his own, tell him "Good down." Pups that are not good about being handled learn better by having food lowered in front of them. A dog that trusts you can be gently guided into position. When you give the command "Down," be sure to say it sweetly!

---

leash right above his collar in your left hand. Have an extra-special treat, such as a small piece of cooked chicken or hot dog, in your right hand. Place it at the end of the pup's nose and steadily move your hand down and forward along the ground. Hold the leash to prevent a sudden lunge for the food. As the puppy goes into the down position, say "Down" very gently.

The difficulty with this exercise is twofold: it's both the submissive aspect and the fact that most people say the word "Down" as if they were a drill sergeant in charge of recruits! So issue the command sweetly, give him the treat and have the pup maintain the down position for several seconds. If he tries to get up immediately, place your hands on his shoulders and press down gently, giving him a very quiet "Good dog." As you progress with this lesson, increase the "down time" until he will hold it until you say "Okay" (his cue for release). Practice this one in the house at various times throughout the day.

By increasing the length of time during which the dog must maintain the down position, you'll find many uses for it. For example, he can lie at your feet in the vet's office or anywhere that both of you have to wait, when you are on the phone, while the family is eating and so forth. If

sit/stay each time until the dog can hold it for at least 30 seconds without moving. After about a week of success, move out on your right foot and take two steps before turning to face the dog. Give the "Stay" hand signal (left palm back toward the dog's head) as you leave. He gets the treat when you return and he holds the sit/stay. Increase the distance that you walk away from him before turning until you reach the length of your training leash. But don't rush it! Go back to the beginning if he moves before he should. No matter what the lesson, never be upset by having to back up for a few days. The repetition and practice are what will make your dog reliable in these commands. It won't do any good to move on to something more difficult if the command is not mastered at the easier levels. Above all, even if

Lead training reinforces the puppy's trust and confidence in you as the leader. Since walking will be a major part of your puppy's house-training procedure, it is helpful to initiate this training before you begin teaching commands.

you progress to training for competitive obedience, he'll already be all set for the exercise called the "long down."

THE SIT/STAY EXERCISE
To teach the sit/stay, have the dog sit on your left side. Hold the leash at waist level in your left hand and let the dog know that you have a treat in your closed right hand. Step forward on your right foot as you say "Stay." Immediately turn and stand directly in front of the dog, keeping your right hand up high so he'll keep his eye on the treat hand and maintain the sit position for a count of five. Return to your original position and offer the reward.

Increase the length of the

OKAY!
This is the signal that tells your dog that he can quit whatever he was doing. Use "Okay" to end a session on a correct response to a command. (Never end on an incorrect response.) Lots of praise follows. People use "Okay" a lot and it has other uses for dogs, too. Your dog is barking. You say, "Okay! Come!" "Okay" signals him to stop the barking activity and "Come" allows him to come to you for a "Good dog."

you do get frustrated, never let your puppy know! Always keep a positive, upbeat attitude during training, which will transmit to your dog for positive results!

The down/stay is taught in the same way once the dog is completely reliable and steady with the down command. Again, don't rush it. With the dog in the down position on your left side, step out on your right foot as you say "Stay." Return by walking around in back of the dog and into your original position. While you are training, it's okay to murmur something like "Hold on" to encourage him to stay put. When the dog will stay without moving when you are at a distance of 3 or 4 feet, begin to increase the length of time before you return. Be sure he holds the down on your return until you say "Okay." At that point, he gets his treat–just so he'll remember for next time that it's not over until it's over.

THE COME EXERCISE

No command is more important to the safety of your dog than "Come." It is what you should say every single time you see the puppy running toward you: "Binky, come! Good dog." During playtime, run a few feet away from the puppy, turn and tell him to "Come" as he is already running to you. You can go so far as to teach your puppy two things

at once if you squat down and hold out your arms. As the pup gets close to you and you're saying "Good dog," bring your right arm in about waist-high. Now he's also learning the hand signal, an excellent device should you be on the phone when you need to get him to come to you! You'll also both be one step ahead when you enter obedience classes.

Puppies, like children, have

COME AND GET IT!

The come command is your dog's safety signal. Until he is 99% perfect in responding, don't use the come command if you cannot enforce it. Practice on leash with treats or squeakers, or whenever the dog is running to you. Never call him to come to you if he is to be corrected for a misdemeanor. Reward the dog with a treat and happy praise whenever he comes to you.

Heel training follows lead training, requiring that the puppy not only accept the lead but walk in an acceptable manner at the owner's side.

notoriously short attention spans, so don't overdo it with any of the training. Keep each lesson short. Break it up with a quick run around the yard or a ball toss, repeat the lesson and quit as soon as the pup gets it right. That way, you will always end with a "Good dog."

When the puppy responds to your well-timed "Come," try it with the puppy on the training leash. This time, catch him off guard, while he's sniffing a leaf or watching a bird: "Binky, come!" You may have to pause for a split second after his name to be sure you have his attention. If the puppy shows any sign of confusion, give the leash a mild jerk and take a couple of steps backward. Do not repeat the command. In this case, as he reaches you, you should say "Good come!"

That's the number-one rule of

training. Each command word is given just once. Anything more is nagging. You'll also notice that all commands are one word only. Even when they are actually two words, you say them as one.

Never call the dog to come to you—with or without his name— if you are angry or intend to correct him for some misbehavior. When correcting the pup, you go to him. Your dog must always connect "Come" with something pleasant and with your approval; then you can rely on his response. Life isn't perfect and neither are puppies. A time will come, often around 10 months of age, when he'll become "selectively deaf" or choose to "forget" his name. He may respond by wagging his tail (and even seeming to smile at you) with a look that says "Make me!" Laugh, throw his favorite toy and skip the lesson you had planned. Pups will be pups!

LET'S GO!
Many people use "Let's go" instead of "Heel" when teaching their dogs to behave on lead. It sounds like more fun! When beginning to teach the heel, whatever command you use, always step off on your left foot. That's the one next to the dog, who is on your left side, in case you've forgotten. Keep a loose leash. When the dog pulls ahead, stop, bring him back and begin again. Use treats to guide him around turns.

THE HEEL EXERCISE

The second most important command to teach, after the come, is the heel. When you are walking your growing puppy, you need to be in control. Besides, it looks terrible to be pulled and yanked down the street, and it's not much fun either! Your eight-to ten-week old puppy will probably follow you everywhere, but that's his natural instinct, not your control over the situation. However, any time he does follow you, you can say "Heel" and be ahead of the game, as he will learn to associate this command with the action of following you before you even begin teaching him to heel.

There is a very precise, almost military, procedure for teaching your dog to heel. As with all obedience training, begin with the dog on your left side. He will be in a very nice sit and you will have the training leash across your chest. Hold the loop and folded leash in your right hand. Pick up the slack leash above the dog in your left hand and hold it loosely at your side. Step out on your left foot as you say "Heel." If the puppy does not move, give a gentle tug or pat your left leg to get him started. If he surges ahead of you, stop and pull him back gently until he is at your side. Tell him to sit and begin again.

Walk a few steps and stop

A Great Pyrenees must be properly heel trained for daily walks as well as for exhibiting in the show ring. Practicing the Pyr's gaiting on the end of a loose lead is ideal for promising show dogs.

while the puppy is correctly beside you. Tell him to sit and give mild verbal praise. (More enthusiastic praise will encourage him to think the lesson is over.) Repeat the lesson, only increasing the number of steps you take as long as the dog is heeling nicely beside you. When you end the lesson, have him hold the sit, then give him the "Okay" to let him know that this is the end of the

Keep training sessions brief and interesting. Great Pyrenees bore more quickly than many other breeds.

MORE PRAISE, LESS FOOD

As you progress with your puppy's lessons, and the puppy is responding well, gradually begin to withhold treats, weaning the puppy off the treats by alternating the treats with times when you offer only verbal praise or a few pats on the dog's side. (Pats on the head are dominant actions and he won't think they are meant to be praise.) Every lesson should end with the puppy's performing the correct action for that session's command. When he gets it right and you withhold the treat, the praise can be as long and lavish as you like. The commands are one word only, but your verbal praise can use as many words as you want...don't skimp!

lesson. Praise him so that he knows he did a good job.

The cure for excessive pulling (a common problem) is to stop when the dog is no more than 2 or 3 feet ahead of you. Guide him back into position and begin again. With a really determined puller, try switching to a head collar. This will automatically turn the pup's head toward you so you can bring him back easily to the heel position. Give quiet, reassuring praise every time the leash goes slack and he's staying with you.

Staying and heeling can take a lot out of a dog, so provide playtime and free-running exercise when the lessons are over to shake off the stress. You don't want him to associate training with all work and no fun.

TRAINING FOR OTHER ACTIVITIES

Once your dog has basic obedience under his collar, and is 12 months of age, you can enter the world of agility training. Dogs think agility is pure fun, like being turned loose in an amusement park full of obstacles! In addition to agility, there are hunting activities for sporting dogs, lure-coursing events for sighthounds, go-to-ground events for terriers, racing for the Nordic sled dogs, herding trials for the shepherd breeds and tracking, which is open to all "nosey" dogs (which would include all dogs!). For those who like to volunteer, there is the wonderful feeling of owning a Therapy Dog and visiting hospices, nursing homes and veterans' homes to bring smiles, comfort and companionship to those who live there.

Around the house, your dog can be taught to do some simple chores. You might teach him to carry a basket of household items or to fetch the morning newspaper. The kids can teach the dog all kinds of tricks, from playing hide-and-seek to balancing a biscuit on his nose. A family dog is what rounds out the family. Everything he does beyond sitting in your lap or gazing lovingly at you represents the bonus of owning a dog.

HEALTHCARE OF YOUR

GREAT PYRENEES

By Lowell Ackerman DVM, DACVD

HEALTHCARE FOR A LIFETIME

When you own a dog, you become his healthcare advocate over his entire lifespan, as well as being the one to shoulder the financial burden of such care. Accordingly, it is worthwhile to focus on prevention rather than treatment, as you and your pet will both be happier.

Of course, the best place to have begun your program of preventative healthcare is with the initial purchase or adoption of your dog. There is no way of guaranteeing that your new furry friend is free of medical problems, but there are some things you can do to improve your odds. You certainly should have done adequate research into the Great Pyrenees and selected your puppy carefully rather than buying on impulse. Health issues aside, a large number of pet abandonment and relinquishment cases arise from a mismatch between pet needs and owner expectations. This is entirely preventable with appropriate planning and finding a good breeder.

Regarding healthcare issues specifically, it is very difficult to

make blanket statements about where to acquire a problem-free pet, but, again, a reputable breeder is your best bet. In an ideal situation, you have the opportunity to see both parents, get references from other owners of the breeder's pups and see genetic-testing documentation for several generations of the litter's ancestors. At the very least, you must thoroughly investigate the Great Pyrenees and the problems inherent in that breed, as well as the genetic testing available to screen for those problems. Genetic testing offers some important benefits, but testing is only available for a few disorders

Recognize the signs of good health on a growing Great Pyrenees.

Facing page: The Great Pyrenees relies upon his owner for his continued good health. In addition to a balanced diet, exercise and proper care, qualified veterinary attention is a vital component to the dog's well-being.

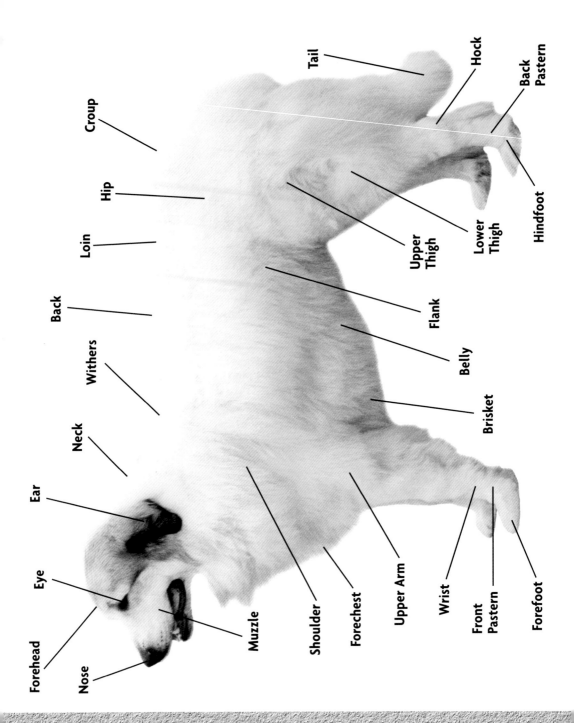

Tail

Hock

Back Pastern

Croup

Hip

Upper Thigh

Lower Thigh

Hindfoot

Loin

Back

Flank

Withers

Belly

Neck

Brisket

Ear

Eye

Forehead

Nose

Muzzle

Shoulder

Forechest

Upper Arm

Wrist

Front Pastern

Forefoot

PHYSICAL STRUCTURE OF THE GREAT PYRENEES

in a relatively small number of breeds and is not available for some of the most common genetic diseases, such as hip dysplasia, cataracts, epilepsy, cardiomyopathy, etc. This area of research is indeed exciting and increasingly important, and advances will continue to be made each year. In fact, recent research has shown that there is an equivalent dog gene for 75% of known human genes, so research done in either species is likely to benefit the other.

We've also discussed that evaluating your chosen pup's behavioral nature and that of his immediate family members is an important part of the selection process that cannot be underestimated or overemphasized. It is sometimes difficult to evaluate temperament in puppies because certain behavioral tendencies, such as some forms of aggression, may not be immediately evident. More dogs are euthanized each year for behavioral reasons than for all medical conditions combined, so it is critical to take temperament issues seriously. Start with a well-balanced, friendly companion and put the time and effort into proper socialization, and you will both be rewarded with a lifelong valued relationship.

With a pup from healthy, sound stock, you become responsible for helping your veteri-

narian keep your pet healthy. Some crucial things happen before you even bring your puppy home. Parasite control typically begins at two weeks of age and vaccinations typically begin at six to eight weeks of age. A prepubertal evaluation is typically scheduled for about six months of age. At this time, a dental evaluation is done (since the adult teeth are now in), heartworm prevention is started and neutering or spaying is most commonly done.

It is critical to commence regular dental care at home if you have not already done so. It may not sound so important, but most dogs have active periodontal disease by four years of age if they don't have their teeth cleaned regularly at home, not just at their veterinary exams. Dental problems lead to more than just bad "doggie breath":

PARASITES
Parasites are nasty little critters that live in or on your dog or puppy. Most puppies are born with roundworms, which are acquired from dormant roundworms residing in the dam. Other parasites can be acquired through contact with infected fecal matter. Take a stool sample to your vet for testing. He will prescribe a safe wormer to treat any parasites found in your puppy's stool. Always have a fecal test performed at your puppy's annual veterinary exam.

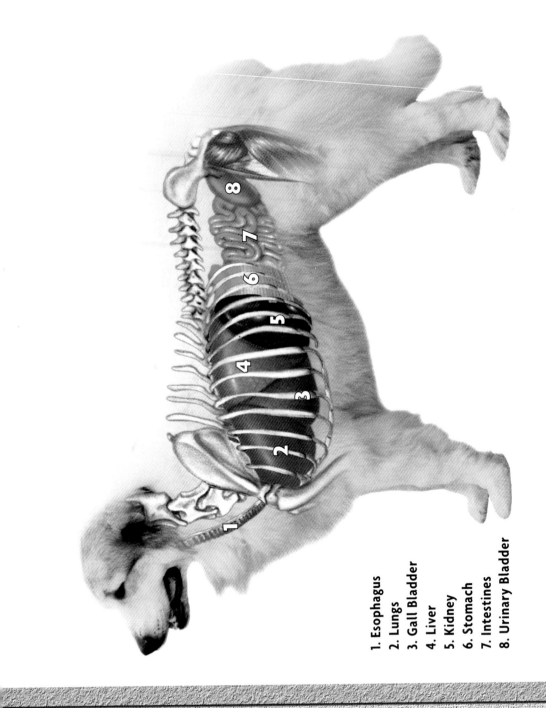

1. Esophagus
2. Lungs
3. Gall Bladder
4. Liver
5. Kidney
6. Stomach
7. Intestines
8. Urinary Bladder

INTERNAL ORGANS OF THE GREAT PYRENEES

gum disease can have very serious medical consequences. If you start brushing your dog's teeth and using antiseptic rinses from a young age, your dog will be accustomed to it and will not resist. The results will be healthy dentition, which your pet will need to enjoy a long, healthy life.

Most dogs are considered adults at a year of age, although Great Pyrenees still have some filling out to do up to about two or so years old. Each breed has different healthcare requirements, so work with your veterinarian to determine what will be needed and what your role should be. This doctor-client relationship is important, because as vaccination guidelines change there may not be an annual "vaccine visit" scheduled. You must make sure that you see your veterinarian at least annually, even if no vaccines are due, because this is the best opportunity to coordinate healthcare activities and to make sure that no medical issues creep by unaddressed.

When your pet reaches three-quarters of his anticipated lifespan, he is considered a "senior" and likely requires some special care. In general, if you've been taking great care of your canine companion throughout his formative and adult years, the transition to senior status should be a smooth one. Age is not a

SAMPLE VACCINATION SCHEDULE

6-8 weeks of age	Parvovirus, Distemper, Adenovirus-2 (Hepatitis)
9-11 weeks of age	Parvovirus, Distemper, Adenovirus-2 (Hepatitis)
12-14 weeks of age	Parvovirus, Distemper, Adenovirus-2 (Hepatitis)
12-16 weeks of age	Rabies
1 year of age	Parvovirus, Distemper, Adenovirus-2 (Hepatitis), Rabies

Revaccination is performed every one to three years, depending on the product, the method of administration and the patient's risk. Initial adult inoculation (for dogs at least 16 weeks of age in which a puppy series was not done or could not be confirmed) is two vaccinations, done three to four weeks apart, with revaccination according to the same criteria mentioned. Other vaccines are given as decided between owner and veterinarian.

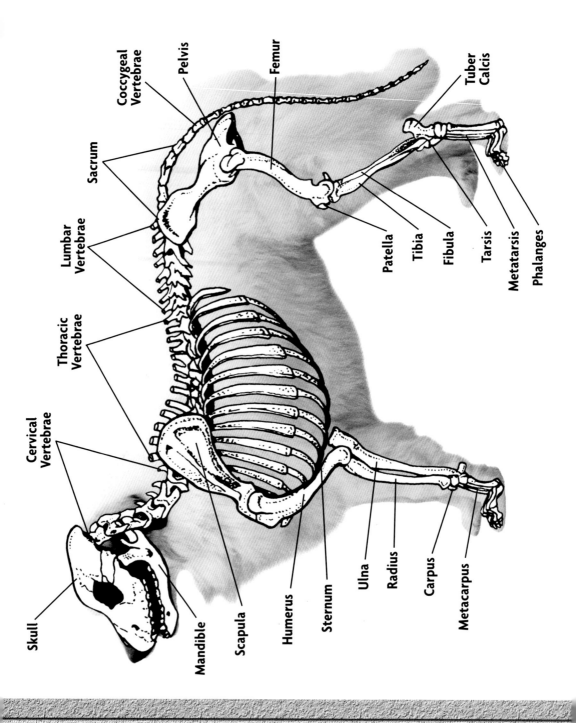

Coccygeal Vertebrae

Pelvis

Femur

Tuber Calcis

Sacrum

Patella

Tibia

Fibula

Tarsis

Metatarsis

Phalanges

Lumbar Vertebrae

Thoracic Vertebrae

Cervical Vertebrae

Skull

Mandible

Scapula

Humerus

Sternum

Ulna

Radius

Carpus

Metacarpus

SKELETAL STRUCTURE OF THE GREAT PYRENEES

disease, and as long as everything is functioning as it should, there is no reason why most of late adulthood should not be rewarding for both you and your pet. This is especially true if you have tended to the details, such as regular veterinary visits, proper dental care, excellent nutrition and management of bone and joint issues.

At this stage in life, your veterinarian may want to schedule visits twice yearly, instead of once, to run some laboratory screenings, electrocardiograms and the like, and to change the diet to something more digestible. Catching problems early is the best way to manage them effectively. Treating the early stages of heart disease is so much easier than trying to intervene when there is more significant damage to the heart muscle. Similarly, managing the beginning of kidney problems is fairly routine if there is no significant kidney damage. Other problems, like cognitive dysfunction (similar to senility and Alzheimer's disease), cancer, diabetes and arthritis, are more common in older dogs but all can be treated to help the dog live as many happy, comfortable years as possible. Just as in people, medical management is more effective (and less expensive) when you catch things early.

ARE VACCINATIONS NECESSARY?

Vaccinations are recommended for all puppies by the American Veterinary Medical Association (AVMA). Some vaccines are absolutely necessary, while others depend upon a dog's or puppy's individual exposure to certain diseases or the animal's immune history. According to the law, rabies vaccinations are required in all 50 states. Some diseases are fatal while others are treatable, making the need for vaccinating against the latter questionable. Follow your veterinarian's recommendations to keep your dog fully immunized and protected. You can also review the AVMA directive on vaccinations on their website: www.avma.org.

SELECTING A VETERINARIAN

There is probably no more important decision that you will make regarding your pet's healthcare than the selection of his doctor. Your pet's veterinarian will be a pediatrician, family-practice physician and gerontologist, depending on the dog's life stage, and will be the individual who makes recommendations regarding issues such as when specialists need to be consulted, when diagnostic testing and/or therapeutic intervention is needed and when you will need to seek outside emergency and critical-care services. Your vet will act as your advocate and liaison throughout these processes.

Everyone has his own idea about what to look for in a vet, an individual who will play a big role in his dog's (and, of course, his own) life for many years to come. For some, it is the compassionate caregiver with whom they hope to develop a professional relationship to span the lifetime of their dogs and even their future pets. For others, they are seeking a clinician with keen diagnostic and therapeutic insight who can deliver state-of-the-art health-care. Still others need a veterinary facility that is open evenings and weekends, or is in close proximity, or provides mobile veterinary services, to accommodate their schedules; these people may not much mind that their dogs might see different veterinarians on each visit. Just as we have different reasons for selecting our own healthcare professionals (e.g., covered by insurance plan, expert in field, convenient location, etc.), we should not expect that there is a one-size-fits-all recommendation for selecting a veterinarian and veterinary practice. The best advice is to be honest in your assessment of what you expect from a veterinary practice and to

> **ASK THE VET**
> Help your vet help you become a well-informed dog owner. Don't be shy about becoming involved in your puppy's veterinary care by asking questions and gaining as much knowledge as you can. For starters, ask what shots your puppy is getting and what diseases they prevent, and discuss with your vet the safest way to vaccinate. Find out what is involved in your dog's annual wellness visits. If you plan to spay or neuter, discuss the best age at which to have this done. Start out on the right "paw" with your puppy's vet and develop good communication with him, as he will care for your dog's health throughout the dog's entire life.

conscientiously research the options in your area. You will quickly appreciate that not all veterinary practices are the same and you will be happiest with one that truly meets your needs.

There is another point to be considered in the selection of veterinary services. Not that long ago, a single veterinarian would attempt to manage all medical and surgical issues as they arose. That was often problematic, because veterinarians are trained in many species and many diseases, and it was just impossible for general veterinary practitioners to be experts in every species, every field and every ailment. However, just as in the human healthcare fields, specialization has allowed general practitioners to concentrate on primary healthcare delivery, especially wellness and the prevention of infectious diseases, and to utilize a network of specialists to assist in the management of conditions that require specific expertise and experience. Thus there are now many types of veterinary specialists, including dermatologists, cardiologists, ophthalmologists, surgeons, internists, oncologists, neurologists, behaviorists, criticalists and others to help primary-care veterinarians deal with complicated medical challenges. In most cases, specialists see cases referred by primary-care veterinarians, make diagnoses and set up management plans. From there, the animals' ongoing care is returned to their primary-care veterinarians. This important team approach to your pet's medical-care needs has provided opportunities for advanced care and an unparalleled level of

DISEASE REFERENCE CHART

	WHAT IS IT?	WHAT CAUSES IT?	SYMPTOMS
Leptospirosis	Severe disease that affects the internal organs; can be spread to people.	A bacterium, which is often carried by rodents, that enters through mucous membranes and spreads quickly throughout the body.	Range from fever, vomiting and loss of appetite in less severe cases to shock, irreversible kidney damage and possibly death in most severe cases.
Rabies	Potentially deadly virus that infects warm-blooded mammals.	Bite from a carrier of the virus, mainly wild animals.	1st stage: dog exhibits change in behavior, fear. 2nd stage: dog's behavior becomes more aggressive. 3rd stage: loss of coordination, trouble with bodily functions.
Parvovirus	Highly contagious virus, potentially deadly.	Ingestion of the virus, which is usually spread through the feces of infected dogs.	Most common: severe diarrhea. Also vomiting, fatigue, lack of appetite.
Canine cough	Contagious respiratory infection.	Combination of types of bacteria and virus. Most common: *Bordetella bronchiseptica* bacteria and parainfluenza virus.	Chronic cough.
Distemper	Disease primarily affecting respiratory and nervous system.	Virus that is related to the human measles virus.	Mild symptoms such as fever, lack of appetite and mucus secretion progress to evidence of brain damage, "hard pad."
Hepatitis	Virus primarily affecting the liver.	Canine adenovirus type I (CAV-I). Enters system when dog breathes in particles.	Lesser symptoms include listlessness, diarrhea, vomiting. More severe symptoms include "blue-eye" (clumps of virus in eye).
Coronavirus	Virus resulting in digestive problems.	Virus is spread through infected dog's feces.	Stomach upset evidenced by lack of appetite, vomiting, diarrhea.

HEARTWORM ZONE
Although heartworm cases have been reported in all 48 continental States, the largest threat exists in the Southeast and Mississippi River Valley. The following states have the highest risk factors: Texas, Florida, Louisiana, North Carolina, Georgia, Mississippi, Tennessee, South Carolina, Alabama and Indiana. Discuss the risk factor with your veterinarian to determine your course of prevention for your dog.

veterinary medicine as it is in human medicine. While veterinary costs are a fraction of what the same services cost in the human healthcare arena, it is still difficult to deal with unanticipated medical costs, especially since they can easily creep into hundreds or even thousands of dollars if specialists or emergency services become involved. However, there are ways of managing these risks. The easiest is to buy pet health insurance and realize that its foremost purpose is not to cover routine healthcare visits but rather to serve as an umbrella for those rainy days when your pet needs medical care and you don't want to worry about whether or not you can afford that care.

Pet insurance policies are very cost-effective (and very inexpensive by human health-insurance standards), but make sure that you buy the policy long before you intend to use it (preferably starting in puppyhood, because coverage will exclude pre-existing conditions) and that you are actually buying an indemnity insurance plan from an insurance company that is regulated by your state or province. Many insurance policy look-alikes are actually discount clubs that are only redeemable at specific locations and for

quality to be delivered.

With all of the opportunities for your pet to receive high-quality veterinary medical care, there is another topic that needs to be addressed at the same time—cost. It's been said that you can have excellent healthcare or inexpensive healthcare, but never both; this is as true in specific services. An indemnity plan covers your pet at almost all veterinary, specialty and emergency practices and is an excellent way to manage your pet's ongoing healthcare needs.

VACCINATIONS AND INFECTIOUS DISEASES

There has never been an easier time to prevent a variety of infectious diseases in your dog, but these advances come with a price—choice. Now while it may seem that choice is a good thing (and it is), it has never been more difficult for the pet owner (or the veterinarian) to make an informed decision about the best way to protect pets through vaccination.

Years ago, it was just accepted that puppies got a starter series of vaccinations and then annual "boosters" throughout their lives to keep them protected. As more and more vaccines became available, consumers wanted the convenience of having all of that protection in a single injection. The result was "multivalent" vaccines that crammed a lot of protection into a single syringe. The manufacturers' recommendations were to give the vaccines annually, and this was a simple enough protocol to follow. However, as veterinary medicine has become more sophisticated and we have started looking

more at healthcare quandaries rather than convenience, it became necessary to reevaluate the situation and deal with some tough questions. It is important to realize that whether or not to use a particular vaccine depends on the risk of contracting the disease against which it protects, the severity of the disease if it is contracted, the duration of immunity provided by the vaccine, the safety of the product and the needs of the individual animal. In a very general sense, rabies, distemper, hepatitis and parvovirus are considered core vaccine needs, while parainfluenza, *Bordetella bronchiseptica*, leptospirosis, coronavirus and borreliosis (Lyme disease) are considered non-core needs and best reserved for animals that demonstrate reasonable risk of contracting the diseases.

NEUTERING/SPAYING

Sterilization procedures (neutering for males/spaying for females) are meant to accomplish several purposes. While the underlying premise is to address the risk of pet overpopulation, there are also some medical and behavioral benefits to the surgeries as well. For females, spaying prior to the first estrus (heat cycle) leads to a marked reduction in the risk of mammary cancer. There are also no manifestations of "heat" to attract male dogs or bleeding in the house. For males, there is prevention of testicular cancer and a reduction in the risk of prostate problems. In both sexes,

there may be some limited reduction in aggressive behaviors toward other dogs, and some diminishing of urine marking, roaming and mounting.

While neutering and spaying do indeed prevent animals from contributing to pet overpopulation, even no-cost and low-cost neutering options have not eliminated the problem. Perhaps one of the main reasons for this is that individuals who intentionally breed their dogs and those who allow their animals to run at large are the main causes of unwanted offspring. Also, animals in shelters are often there because they were abandoned or relinquished, not because they came from unplanned matings. Neutering/spaying is important, but it should be considered in the context of the real causes of animals' ending up in shelters and eventually being euthanized.

One of the important considerations regarding neutering is that it is a surgical procedure. This sometimes gets lost in discussions of low-cost procedures and commoditization of the process. In females, spaying is specifically referred to as an ovariohysterectomy. In this procedure, a midline incision is made in the abdomen and the entire uterus and both ovaries are surgically removed. While this is a major invasive surgical procedure, it usually has few complications, because it is typically performed on young healthy animals. However, it is a major surgery, as any woman who has had a hysterectomy will attest.

In males, neutering has traditionally referred to castration, which involves the surgical removal of both testicles. While still a significant piece of surgery, there is not the abdominal exposure that is required in the female surgery. In addition, there is now a chemical sterilization option, in which a solution is injected into each testicle, leading to atrophy of the sperm-producing cells. This can typically be done under sedation rather than full anesthesia. This is a relatively new approach, and there are no long-term clinical studies yet available.

Neutering/spaying is typically done around six months of age at most veterinary hospitals, although techniques have been pioneered to perform the procedures in animals as young as eight weeks of age. In general, the surgeries on the very young animals are done for the specific reason of sterilizing them before they go to their new homes. This is done in some shelter hospitals for assurance that the animals will definitely not produce any pups.

Otherwise, these organizations need to rely on owners to comply with their wishes to have the animals "altered" at a later date, something that does not always happen.

There are some exciting immunocontraceptive "vaccines" currently under development, and there may be a time when contraception in pets will not require surgical procedures. We anxiously await these developments.

SPAY'S THE WAY

Although spaying a female dog qualifies as major surgery—an ovariohysterectomy, in fact—this procedure is regarded as routine when performed by a qualified veterinarian on a healthy dog. The advantages to spaying a bitch are many and great. Spayed dogs do not develop uterine cancer or any life-threatening diseases of the genitals. Likewise, spayed dogs are at a significantly reduced risk of breast cancer. Bitches (and owners) are relieved of the regular demands of heat cycles. A spayed bitch will not leave bloody stains on your furniture during estrus and you will not have to contend with single-minded macho males trying to climb your fence in order to seduce your bitch. The spayed bitch's coat will not show the ill effects of her estrogen level's climbing such as a dull, lackluster outer coat or patches of hairlessness.

S. E. M. BY DR. DENNIS KUNKEL, UNIVERSITY OF HAWAII.

A scanning electron micrograph of a dog flea, *Ctenocephalides canis*, on dog hair.

EXTERNAL PARASITES

FLEAS

Fleas have been around for millions of years and, while we have better tools now for controlling them than at any time in the past, there still is little chance that they will end up on an endangered species list. Actually, they are very well adapted to living on our pets, and they continue to adapt as we make advances.

The female flea can consume 15 times her weight in blood during active reproduction and can lay as many as 40 eggs a day. These eggs are very resistant to the effects of insecticides. They hatch into larvae, which then mature and spin cocoons. The immature fleas reside in this pupal stage until the time is right for feeding. This pupal stage is also very resistant to the effects of insecticides, and pupae can last in the environment without feeding for many months. Newly emergent fleas are attracted to animals by the warmth of the animals' bodies, movement and exhaled carbon dioxide. However, when they first emerge from their cocoons, they orient towards light; thus when an animal passes between a flea and the light source, casting a shadow, the flea pounces and starts to feed. If the animal turns out to be a dog or cat, the reproductive cycle continues. If the flea lands on another type of animal, including a person, the flea will bite but will then look for a more appropriate host. An emerging adult flea can survive without feeding for up to 12 months, but once it tastes blood it can only survive off its host for three to four days.

It was once thought that fleas spend most of their lives in the environment, but we now know that fleas won't willingly jump off a dog unless leaping to another dog or when physically removed by brushing, bathing or other manipulation. Flea eggs, on the other hand, are shiny and smooth, and they roll off the animal and into the environment. The eggs, larvae and pupae then exist in the environment, but once the adult finds a susceptible animal, it's home sweet home until the flea is convinced to seek refuge elsewhere.

Since adult fleas live on the animal and immature forms survive in the environment, a successful treatment plan must address all stages of the flea life cycle. There are now several safe and effective flea-control products that can be applied on a monthly

FLEA PREVENTION FOR YOUR DOG
- Discuss with your veterinarian the safest product to protect your dog, likely in the form of a monthly tablet or a liquid preparation placed on the back of the dog's neck.
- For dogs suffering from flea-bite dermatitis, a shampoo or topical insecticide treatment is required.
- Your lawn and property should be sprayed with an insecticide designed to kill fleas and ticks that lurk outdoors.
- Using a flea comb, check the dog's coat regularly for any signs of parasites.
- Practice good housekeeping: vacuum floors, carpets and furniture regularly, especially in the areas that the dog frequents, and wash the dog's bedding weekly.
- Follow up house-cleaning with carpet shampoos and sprays to rid the house of fleas at all stages of development. Insect growth regulators are the safest option.

basis. These include fipronil, imidacloprid, selamectin and permethrin (found in several formulations). Most of these products have significant flea-killing rates within 24 hours. However, none of them will control the immature forms in the environment. To accomplish this, there are a variety of insect growth regulators that can be

THE FLEA'S LIFE CYCLE

What came first, the flea or the egg? This age-old mystery is more difficult to comprehend than the actual cycle of the flea. Fleas usually live only about four months. A female can lay 2,000 eggs in her lifetime.

Egg

After ten days of rolling around your carpet or under your furniture, the eggs hatch into larvae, which feed on various and sundry debris. In days or months, depending on the climate, the larvae spin a cocoon and develop into the pupal or nymph stage, which quickly develop into fleas.

Larva

Pupa

These immature fleas must locate a host within 10 to 14 days or they will die. Only about 1% of the flea population exist as adult fleas, while the other 99% exist as eggs, larvae or pupae.

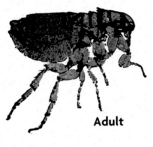

Adult

KILL FLEAS THE NATURAL WAY

If you choose not to go the route of conventional medication, there are some natural ways to ward off fleas:

- Dust your dog with a natural flea powder, composed of such herbal goodies as rosemary, wormwood, pennyroyal, citronella, rue, tobacco powder and eucalyptus.
- Apply diatomaceous earth, the fossilized remains of single-cell algae, to your carpets, furniture and pet's bedding. Even though it's not good for dogs, it's even worse for fleas, which will dry up swiftly and die.
- Brush your dog frequently, give him adequate exercise and let him fast occasionally. All of these activities strengthen the dog's system and make him more resistant to disease and parasites.
- Bathe your dog with a capful of pennyroyal or eucalyptus oil.
- Feed a natural diet, free of additives and preservatives. Add some fresh garlic and brewer's yeast to the dog's morning portion, as these items have flea-repelling properties.

sprayed into the environment (e.g., pyriproxyfen, methoprene, fenoxycarb) as well as insect development inhibitors such as lufenuron that can be administered. These compounds have no effect on adult fleas, but they stop immature forms from developing into adults. In years gone by, we relied heavily on toxic insecticides (such as organophosphates, organochlorines and carbamates) to manage the flea problem, but today's options are not only much safer to use on our pets but also safer for the environment.

TICKS

Ticks are members of the spider class (arachnids) and are blood-sucking parasites capable of transmitting a variety of diseases, including Lyme disease, ehrlichiosis, babesiosis and Rocky Mountain spotted fever. It's easy to see ticks on your own skin, but it is more of a challenge when your furry companion is affected. Whenever you happen to be planning a stroll in a tick-infested area (especially forests, grassy or wooded areas or parks) be prepared to do a thorough inspection of your dog afterward to search for ticks. Ticks can be tricky, so make sure you spend time looking in the ears, between the toes and everywhere else where a tick might hide. Ticks need to be attached for 24–72 hours before they transmit most of the diseases that they carry, so you do have a window of opportunity for some preventative intervention.

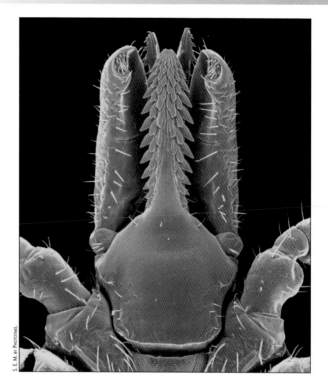

S. E. M. BY PHOTOTAKE.

A scanning electron micrograph of the head of a female deer tick, *Ixodes dammini*, a parasitic tick that carries Lyme disease.

A TICKING BOMB

There is nothing good about a tick's harpooning his nose into your dog's skin. Among the diseases caused by ticks are Rocky Mountain spotted fever, canine ehrlichiosis, canine babesiosis, canine hepatozoonosis and Lyme disease. If a dog is allergic to the saliva of a female wood tick, he can develop tick paralysis.

Female ticks live to eat and breed. They can lay between 4,000 and 5,000 eggs and they die soon after. Males, on the other hand, live only to mate with the females and continue the process as long as they are able. Most ticks live on multiple hosts before parasitizing dogs. The immature forms typically reside on grass and shrubs, waiting for susceptible animals to walk by. The larvae and nymph stages typically feed on wildlife.

If only a few ticks are present on a dog, they can be plucked out, but it is important to remove the entire head and mouthparts,

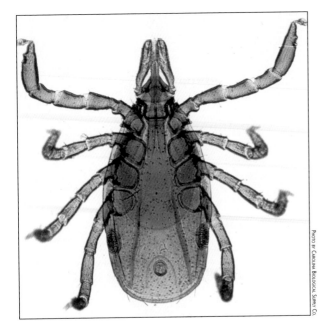

PHOTO BY CAROLINA BIOLOGICAL SUPPLY CO.

Deer tick, Ixodes dammini.

disposed of in a container of alcohol or flushed down the toilet.

Some of the newer flea products, specifically those with fipronil, selamectin and permethrin, have effect against some, but not all, species of tick. Flea collars containing appropriate insecticides (e.g., propoxur, chlorfenvinphos) can aid in tick control. In most areas, such collars should be placed on animals in March, at the beginning of the tick season, and changed regularly. Leaving the collar on when the insecticide level is waning invites the development of resistance. Amitraz collars are also good for tick control, and the active ingredient does not interfere with other flea-control products. The ingredient helps prevent the attachment of ticks to the skin and will cause those ticks already on the skin to detach themselves.

which may be deeply embedded in the skin. This is best accomplished with forceps designed especially for this purpose; fingers can be used, but should be protected with rubber gloves, plastic wrap or at least a paper towel. The tick should be grasped as closely as possible to the animal's skin and should be pulled upward with steady, even pressure. Do not squeeze, crush or puncture the body of the tick or you risk exposure to any disease carried by that tick. Once the ticks have been removed, the sites of attachment should be disinfected. Your hands should then be washed with soap and water to further minimize risk of contagion. The tick should be

TICK CONTROL

Removal of underbrush and leaf litter and the thinning of trees in areas where tick control is desired are recommended. These actions remove the cover and food sources for small animals that serve as hosts for ticks. With continued mowing of grasses in these areas, the probability of ticks' surviving is further reduced. A variety of insecticide ingredients (e.g., resmethrin, carbaryl, permethrin, chlorpyrifos, dioxathion and allethrin) are registered for tick control around the home.

MITES

Mites are tiny arachnid parasites that parasitize the skin of dogs. Skin diseases caused by mites are referred to as "mange," and there are many different forms seen in dogs. These forms are very different from one another, each one warranting an individual description.

Sarcoptic mange, or scabies, is one of the itchiest conditions that affect dogs. The microscopic *Sarcoptes* mites burrow into the superficial layers of the skin and can drive dogs crazy with itchiness. They are also communicable to people, although they can't complete their reproductive cycle on people. Not only are the mites tiny but also are often difficult to find when trying to make a diagnosis. Skin scrapings from multiple areas are examined microscopically but, even then, sometimes the mites cannot be found.

Fortunately, scabies is relatively easy to treat, and there are a variety of products that will successfully kill the mites. Since the mites can't live in the environment for very long without feeding, a complete cure is usually possible within four to eight weeks.

Cheyletiellosis is caused by a relatively large mite, which sometimes can be seen even without a microscope. Often referred to as "walking dandruff," this also causes itching, but not usually as profound as with scabies.

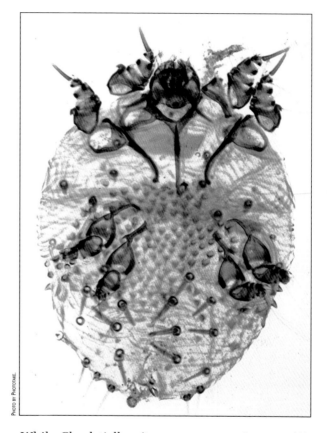

PHOTO BY PHOTOTAKE.

Sarcoptes scabiei, commonly known as the "itch mite."

While *Cheyletiella* mites can survive somewhat longer in the environment than scabies mites, they too are relatively easy to treat, being responsive not only to the medications used to treat scabies but also often to flea-control products.

Otodectes cynotis is the cause of ear mites and is one of the more common causes of mange, especially in young dogs in shelters or pet stores. That's because the mites are typically present in large numbers and are quickly spread to

Micrograph of a dog louse, *Heterodoxus spiniger*. Female lice attach their eggs to the hairs of the dog. As the eggs hatch, the larval lice bite and feed on the blood. Lice can also feed on dead skin and hair. This feeding activity can cause hair loss and skin problems.

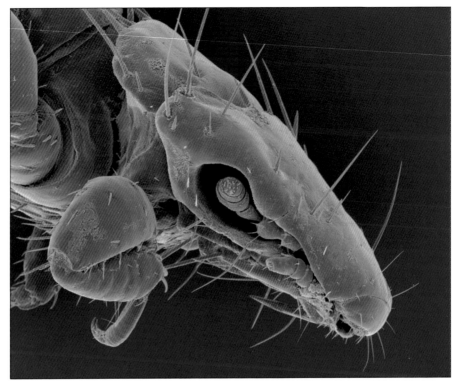

S. E. M. BY DR. DENNIS KUNKEL, UNIVERSITY OF HAWAII

nearby animals. The mites rarely do much harm but can be difficult to eradicate if the treatment regimen is not comprehensive. While many try to treat the condition with ear drops only, this is the most common cause of treatment failure. Ear drops cause the mites to simply move out of the ears and as far away as possible (usually to the base of the tail) until the insecticide levels in the ears drop to an acceptable level—then it's back to business as usual! The successful treatment of ear mites requires treating all animals in the household with a systemic insecticide, such as selamectin, or a combination of miticidal ear drops combined with whole-body flea-control preparations.

Demodicosis, sometimes referred to as red mange, can be one of the most difficult forms of mange to treat. Part of the problem has to do with the fact that the mites live in the hair follicles and are relatively well shielded from topical and systemic products. The main issue, however, is that demodectic mange typically only results when there is some underlying process interfering with the dog's immune system.

Since *Demodex* mites are normal residents of the skin of

mammals, including humans, there is usually only a mite population explosion when the immune system fails to keep the number of mites in check. In young animals, the immune deficit may be transient or it may reflect an actual inherited immune problem. In older animals, demodicosis is usually seen only when there is another disease hampering the immune system, such as diabetes, cancer, thyroid problems or the use of immune-suppressing drugs. Accordingly, treatment involves not only trying to kill the mange mites but also discerning what is interfering with immune function and correcting it if possible.

Chiggers represent several different species of mite that don't parasitize dogs specifically, but do latch on to passersby and can cause irritation. The problem is most prevalent in wooded areas in the late summer and fall. Treatment is not difficult, as the mites do not complete their life cycle on dogs and are susceptible to a variety of insecticides.

MOSQUITOES

Mosquitoes have long been known to transmit a variety of diseases to people, as well as just being biting pests during warm weather. They also pose a real risk to pets. Not only do they carry deadly heartworms but

recently there also has been much concern over their involvement with West Nile virus. While we can avoid heartworm with the use of preventive medications, there are no such preventives for West Nile virus. The only method of prevention in endemic areas is active mosquito control. Fortunately, most dogs that have been exposed to the virus only developed flu-like symptoms and, to date, there have not been the large number of reported deaths in canines as seen in some other species.

Illustration of *Demodex folliculoram.*

MOSQUITO REPELLENT

Low concentrations of DEET (less than 10%), found in many human mosquito repellents, have been safely used in dogs but, in these concentrations, probably give only about two hours of protection. DEET may be safe in these small concentrations, but since it is not licensed for use on dogs, there is no research proving its safety for dogs. Products containing permethrin give the longest-lasting protection, perhaps two to four weeks. As DEET is not licensed for use on dogs, and both DEET and permethrin can be quite toxic to cats, appropriate care should be exercised. Other products, such as those containing oil of citronella, also have some mosquito-repellent activity, but typically have a relatively short duration of action.

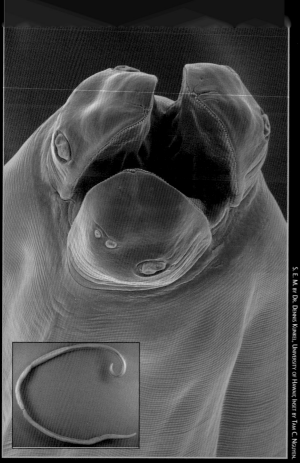

ASCARID DANGERS

The most commonly encountered worms in dogs are roundworms known as ascarids. *Toxascaris leonine* and *Toxocara canis* are the two species that infect dogs. Subsisting in the dog's stomach and intestines, adult roundworms can grow to 7 inches in length and adult females can lay in excess of 200,000 eggs in a single day.

In humans, visceral larval migrans affects people who have ingested eggs of *Toxocara canis*, which frequently contaminates children's sandboxes, beaches and park grounds. The roundworms reside in the human's stomach and intestines, as they would in a dog's, but do not mature. Instead, they find their way to the liver, lungs and skin, or even to the heart or kidneys in severe cases. Deworming puppies is critical in preventing the infection in humans, and young children should never handle nursing pups who have not been dewormed.

The ascarid roundworm *Toxocara canis*, showing the mouth with three lips. Inset: Photomicrograph of the roundworm *Ascaris lumbricoides*.

INTERNAL PARASITES: WORMS

ASCARIDS

Ascarids are intestinal roundworms that rarely cause severe disease in dogs. Nonetheless, they are of major public health significance because they can be transferred to people. Sadly, it is children who are most commonly affected by the parasite, probably from inadvertently ingesting ascarid-contaminated soil. In fact, many yards and children's sandboxes contain appreciable numbers of ascarid eggs. So, while ascarids don't bite dogs or latch onto their intestines to suck blood, they do cause some nasty medical conditions in children and are best eradicated from our furry friends. Because pups can start passing ascarid eggs by three weeks of age, most parasite-control programs begin at two weeks of age and are repeated every two weeks until pups are eight weeks old. It is important to

HOOKED ON ANCYLOSTOMA

Adult dogs can become infected by the bloodsucking nematodes we commonly call hookworms via ingesting larvae from the ground or via the larvae penetrating the dog's skin. It is not uncommon for infected dogs to show no symptoms of hookworm infestation. Sometimes symptoms occur within ten days of exposure. These symptoms can include bloody diarrhea, anemia, loss of weight and general weakness. Dogs pass the hookworm eggs in their stools, which serves as the vet's method of identifying the infestation. The hookworm larvae can encyst themselves in the dog's tissues and be released when the dog is experiencing stress.

Caused by an *Ancylostoma* species, whose common host is the dog, cutaneous larval migrans affects humans, causing itching and lumps and streaks beneath the surface of the skin.

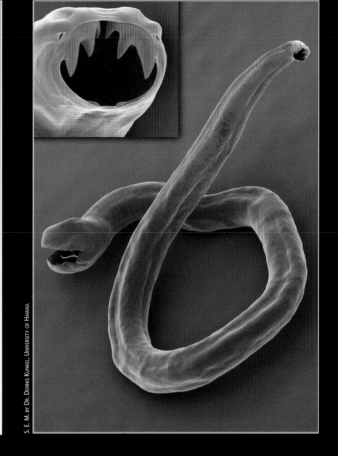

S. E. M. BY DR. DENNIS KUNKEL, UNIVERSITY OF HAWAII.

realize that bitches can pass ascarids to their pups even if they test negative prior to whelping. Accordingly, bitches are best treated at the same time as the pups.

HOOKWORMS

Unlike ascarids, hookworms do latch onto a dog's intestinal tract and can cause significant loss of blood and protein. Similar to ascarids, hookworms can be transmitted to humans, where they cause a condition known as cutaneous larval migrans. Dogs can become infected either by consuming the infective larvae or by the larvae's penetrating the skin directly. People most often get infected when they are lying on the ground (such as on a beach) and the larvae penetrate the skin. Yes, the larvae can penetrate through a beach blanket. Hookworms are typically susceptible to the same medications used to treat ascarids.

The hookworm *Ancylostoma caninum* infects the colon of dogs. Inset: Note the row of hooks at the posterior end, used to anchor the worm to the intestinal wall.

WHIPWORMS

Whipworms latch onto the lower aspects of the dog's colon and can cause cramping and diarrhea. Eggs do not start to appear in the dog's feces until about three months after the dog was infected. This worm has a peculiar life cycle, which makes it more difficult to control than ascarids or hookworms. The good thing is that whipworms rarely are transferred to people.

Some of the medications used to treat ascarids and hookworms are also effective against whipworms, but, in general, a separate treatment protocol is needed. Since most of the medications are effective against the adults but not the eggs or larvae, treatment is typically repeated in three weeks, and then often in three

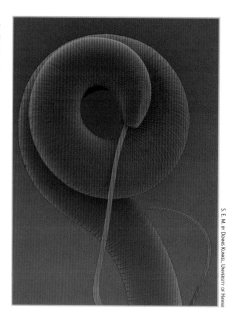

Adult whipworm, *Trichuris* sp., an intestinal parasite.

S. E. M. BY DENNIS KUNKEL, UNIVERSITY OF HAWAII

WORM-CONTROL GUIDELINES

- Practice sanitary habits with your dog and home.
- Clean up after your dog and don't let him sniff or eat other dogs' droppings.
- Control insects and fleas in the dog's environment. Fleas, lice, cockroaches, beetles, mice and rats can act as hosts for various worms.
- Prevent dogs from eating uncooked meat, raw poultry and dead animals.
- Keep dogs and children from playing in sand and soil.
- Kennel dogs on cement or gravel; avoid dirt runs.
- Administer heartworm preventatives regularly.
- Have your vet examine your dog's stools at your annual visits.
- Select a boarding kennel carefully so as to avoid contamination from other dogs or an unsanitary environment.
- Prevent dogs from roaming. Obey local leash laws.

months as well. Unfortunately, since dogs don't develop resistance to whipworms, it is difficult to prevent them from getting reinfected if they visit soil contaminated with whipworm eggs.

TAPEWORMS

There are many different species of tapeworm that affect dogs, but *Dipylidium caninum* is probably the most common and is spread by fleas. Flea larvae feed on organic debris and tapeworm eggs in the environment and, when a dog chews at himself and manages to ingest fleas, he might get a dose of tapeworm at the same time. The tapeworm then develops further in the intestine of the dog.

The tapeworm itself, which latches onto the intestinal wall, is composed of numerous segments. When the segments break off into the intestine (as proglottids), they may accumulate around the rectum, like grains of rice. While this tapeworm is  disgusting in its behavior, it is not directly communicable to humans (although humans can also get infected by swallowing fleas).

A much more dangerous flatworm is *Echinococcus multilocularis*, which is typically found in foxes, coyotes and wolves. The eggs are passed in the feces and infect rodents, and, when dogs eat the rodents, the dogs can be infected by thousands of adult tapeworms. While the parasites don't cause many problems in dogs, this is considered the most lethal worm infection that people can get. Take appropriate precautions if you live in an area in which these tapeworms are found. Do not use mulch that may contain feces of dogs, cats or wildlife, and discourage your pets from hunting

wildlife. Treat these tapeworm infections aggressively in pets, because if humans get infected, approximately half die.

HEARTWORMS

Heartworm disease is caused by the parasite *Dirofilaria immitis* and is seen in dogs around the world. The parasite itself, an actual worm, is spread between dogs by the bite of an infected mosquito. The mosquito injects infective larvae into the dog's skin with its bite, and these larvae develop under the skin for a period of time before making their way to the heart. There they develop into adults, which grow and create blockage of the heart, lungs and major blood vessels there. They also start

Dog tapeworm proglottid (body segment).

The dog tapeworm *Taenia pisiformis*.

S. E. M. BY DR. DENNIS KUNKEL, UNIVERSITY OF HAWAII.

A Look at Internal Parasites

Asacarid *Rhabditis*

Hookworm *Ancylostoma caninum*

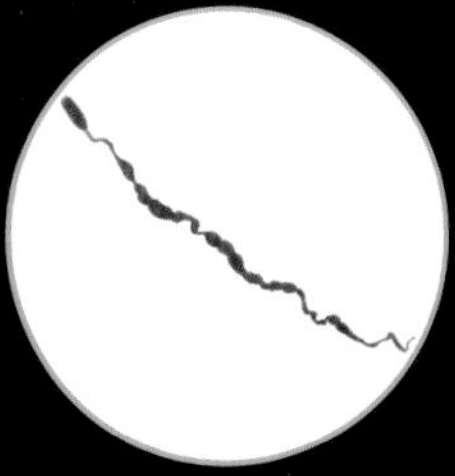

Tapeworm *Dipylidium caninum*

Heartworm *Dirofilaria immitis*

PHOTO BY CAROLINA BIOLOGICAL SUPPLY CO.

PHOTO BY CAROLINA BIOLOGICAL SUPPLY CO.

PHOTO BY TAM C. NGUYEN

PHOTO BY TAM C. NGUYEN

producing offspring (microfilariae) and these microfilariae circulate in the bloodstream, waiting to hitch a ride when the next mosquito bites. Once in the mosquito, the microfilariae develop into infective larvae and the entire process is repeated.

When dogs get infected with heartworm, over time they tend to develop symptoms associated with heart disease, such as coughing, exercise intolerance and potentially many other manifestations. Diagnosis is confirmed by either seeing the microfilariae themselves in blood samples or using immunologic tests (antigen testing) to identify the presence of adult heartworms. Since antigen tests measure the presence of adult heartworms and microfilarial tests measure offspring produced by adults, neither are positive until six to seven months after the initial infection. However, the beginning of damage can occur by fifth-stage larvae as early as three months after infection. Thus it is possible for dogs to be harboring problem-causing larvae for up to three months before either type of test would identify an infection.

The good news is that there are great protocols available for preventing heartworm in dogs. Testing is critical in the process, and it is important to understand the benefits as well as the limitations of such testing. All dogs six months of age or older that have not been on continuous heartworm-preventive

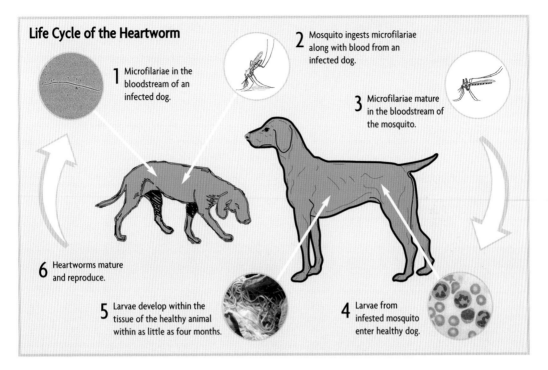

Life Cycle of the Heartworm

1 Microfilariae in the bloodstream of an infected dog.

2 Mosquito ingests microfilariae along with blood from an infected dog.

3 Microfilariae mature in the bloodstream of the mosquito.

4 Larvae from infested mosquito enter healthy dog.

5 Larvae develop within the tissue of the healthy animal within as little as four months.

6 Heartworms mature and reproduce.

medication should be screened with microfilarial or antigen tests. For dogs receiving preventive medication, periodic antigen testing helps assess the effectiveness of the preventives. The American Heartworm Society guidelines suggest that annual retesting may not be necessary when owners have absolutely provided continuous heartworm prevention. Retesting on a two- to three-year interval may be sufficient in these cases. However, your veterinarian will likely have specific guidelines under which heartworm preventives will be prescribed, and many prefer to err on the side of safety and retest annually.

It is indeed fortunate that heartworm is relatively easy to prevent, because treatments can be as life-threatening as the disease itself. Treatment requires a two-step process that kills the adult heartworms first and then the microfilariae. Prevention is obviously preferable; this involves a once-monthly oral or topical treatment. The most common oral preventives include ivermectin (not suitable for some breeds), moxidectin and milbemycin oxime; the once-a-month topical drug selamectin provides heartworm protection in addition to flea, tick and other parasite controls.

In the show ring, the Great Pyrenees sparkles as a snow-white beauty whose days of tackling wolves seem far behind him.

SHOWING YOUR
GREAT PYRENEES

Is dog showing in your blood? Are you excited by the idea of gaiting your handsome Great Pyrenees around the ring to the thunderous applause of an enthusiastic audience? Are you certain that your beloved Great Pyrenees is flawless? You are not alone! Every loving owner thinks that his dog has no faults, or too few to mention. No matter how many times an owner reads over the breed standard, he cannot find any faults in his aristocratic companion dog. If this sounds like you, and if you are considering entering your Great Pyrenees in a dog show, here are some basic questions to ask yourself:

- Did you purchase a "show-quality" puppy from the breeder?
- Is your puppy at least six months of age?
- Does the puppy exhibit correct show type for his breed?
- Does your puppy have any disqualifying faults?
- Is your Great Pyrenees registered with the American Kennel Club?
- How much time do you have to devote to training, grooming, conditioning and exhibiting your dog?

- Do you understand the rules and regulations of a dog show?
- Do you have time to learn how to show your dog properly?
- Do you have the financial resources to invest in showing your dog?
- Will you show the dog yourself or hire a professional handler?
- Do you have a vehicle that can accommodate your weekend trips to the dog shows?
  Success in the show ring

Exhibiting a Great Pyrenees in top condition requires dedication, training and financial commitment.

requires more than a pretty face, a waggy tail and a pocketful of liver. Even though dog shows can be exciting and enjoyable, the sport of conformation makes great demands on the exhibitors and the

HOW THE DOG MEASURES UP

Judges must assess each dog's correct measurements in the show ring, as many breed standards include height disqualifications for dogs that are too short or too tall, along with desired weight ranges. According to the American Kennel Club, "Height is measured from a point horizontal with the withers, straight down to the ground." Although length of body is not described in the breed standard in terms of inches, it is often discussed in relation to the proportional balance of the dog. The AKC states, "Length is measured from point of shoulder to point of buttock."

dogs. Winning exhibitors live for their dogs, devoting time and money to their dogs' presentation, conditioning and training. Very few novices, even those with good dogs, will find themselves in the winners' circle, though it does happen. Don't be disheartened, though. Every exhibitor began as a novice and worked his way up to the Group ring. It's the "working your way up" part that you must keep in mind.

Assuming that you have purchased a puppy of the correct type and quality for showing, let's begin to examine the world of showing and what's required to get started. Although the entry fee into a dog show is nominal, there are lots of other hidden costs involved with "finishing" your Great Pyrenees, that is, making him a champion. Things like equipment, travel, training and conditioning all cost money. A more serious campaign will include fees for a professional handler, boarding, cross-country travel and advertising. Top-winning show dogs represent an investment of over $100,000 per year. Keep in mind that few dog shows offer cash prizes! For the 100,000 reasons listed above, many dog owners are opting to participate in United Kennel Club shows, where professional handlers are not permitted. These shows are more owner-oriented and, for many, more rewarding than AKC events.

Many owners, on the other hand, enter their "average" Great Pyreneess in dog shows for the fun and enjoyment of it. Dog showing makes an absorbing hobby with many rewards for dogs and owners alike. If you're having fun, meeting other people who share your interests and enjoying the overall experience, you likely will catch the "bug." Once the dog-show bug bites, its effects can last a lifetime; it's certainly much better than a deer tick! Soon you will be envisioning yourself in the center ring at the Westminster Kennel Club Dog Show in New York City, competing for the prestigious Best in Show cup. This magical dog show is televised annually from Madison Square Garden, and the victorious dog becomes a celebrity overnight.

Presentation is half the battle at a dog show. Not only must you show your majestic Mountain Dog to his best advantage, you must present yourself as a well-prepared professional.

AKC CONFORMATION SHOWING

GETTING STARTED

Visiting a dog show as a spectator is a great place to start. Pick up the show catalog to find out what time your breed is being shown, who is judging the breed and in what ring the classes will be held. To start, Great Pyreneess compete against other Great Pyreneess, and the winner is selected as Best of Breed by the judge. This is the procedure for each breed. At a group show, all of the Best of Breed winners go on to compete for Group One in their respective group. For example, all Best of Breed winners for each breed in the Working Group compete against each other; this is done for

---

BECOMING A CHAMPION

An official AKC champion of record requires that a dog accumulate 15 points under three different judges, including two "majors" under different judges. Points are awarded based on the number of dogs entered into competition, varying from breed to breed and place to place. A win of three, four or five points is considered a "major." The AKC annually assigns a schedule of points to adjust the variations that accompany a breed's popularity and the population of a given area.

all seven groups. Finally, all seven group winners go head to head in the ring for the Best in Show award.

What most spectators don't understand is the basic idea of conformation. A dog show is often referred as a "conformation" show. This means that the judge should decide how each dog stacks up (conforms) to the breed standard for his given breed: how well does this Great Pyrenees conform to the ideal representative detailed in the standard? Ideally, this is what happens. In reality, however, this ideal often gets slighted as the judge compares Great Pyrenees #1 to Great Pyrenees #2. Again, the ideal is that each dog is judged based on his merits in comparison to his breed standard, not in comparison to the other dogs in the ring. It is easier for judges to compare dogs of the same breed to decide which he thinks is the better specimen; in the Group and Best in Show ring, however, it is very difficult to compare one breed to another, like apples to oranges. Thus, the dog's conformation to the breed standard, not to mention good handling and advertising dollars, is essential to his success.

The breed standard, which is drafted and approved by the breed's national parent club, the Great Pyrenees Club of America, is then submitted to the American

FOR MORE INFORMATION....

For reliable, up-to-date information about registration, dog shows and other canine competitions, contact one of the national registries by mail or via the Internet.

American Kennel Club
5580 Centerview Dr., Raleigh, NC 27606-3390
www.akc.org

United Kennel Club
100 E. Kilgore Road, Kalamazoo, MI 49002
www.ukcdogs.com

Canadian Kennel Club
89 Skyway Ave., Suite 100, Etobicoke, Ontario
M9W 6R4 Canada
www.ckc.ca

The Kennel Club
1-5 Clarges St., Piccadilly, London W1Y 8AB, UK
www.the-kennel-club.org.uk

Kennel Club (AKC). The dog described in the standard is the perfect dog of that breed, and breeders keep their eye on the standard when they choose which dogs to breed, hoping to get closer and closer to the ideal with each litter.

Another good first step for the novice is to join a dog club. You will be astonished by the many and different kinds of dog clubs in the country, with about 5,000 clubs holding events every year. Most clubs require that prospective new members present two letters of recommendation from existing members. Perhaps you've made some friends visiting a show held by a particular club and you would like to join that club. Dog clubs may specialize in a single breed, like a local or regional Great Pyrenees club, or in a specific pursuit, such as obedience, tracking or hunting tests. There are all-breed clubs for all dog enthusiasts, which sponsor special training days, seminars on topics like grooming or handling or lectures on breeding or canine genetics. There are also clubs that specialize in certain types of dogs, like herding dogs, hunting dogs, companion dogs, etc.

A parent club is the national organization, sanctioned by the AKC, which promotes and safeguards its breed in the country. The Great Pyrenees Club of America can be contacted on the Internet at www.clubs.akc.org/gpca/. The parent club holds an annual national specialty show, usually in a different city each year, in which many of the country's top dogs, handlers and breeders gather to compete. At a specialty

show, only members of a single breed are invited to participate. There are also group specialties, in which all members of a Group are invited. For more information about dog clubs in your area, contact the AKC at www.akc.org on the Internet or write them at their Raleigh, NC address.

HOW SHOWS ARE ORGANIZED

Three kinds of conformation shows are offered by the AKC. There is the all-breed show, in which all AKC-recognized breeds can compete; the specialty show, which is for one breed only and usually sponsored by the breed's parent club, and the Group show, for all breeds in one of the seven AKC groups. The Great Pyrenees competes in the Working Group.

For a dog to become an AKC champion of record, the dog must earn 15 points at shows. The points must be awarded by at least three different judges and must include two "majors" under different judges. A "major" is a three-, four- or five-point win, and the number of points per win is determined by the number of dogs competing in the show on that day. Dogs that are absent or are excused are not counted. The number of points that are awarded varies from breed to breed. More dogs are needed to attain a major in more popular breeds, and fewer dogs are needed in less popular breeds. Yearly, the AKC evaluates

If it is your first time in the show ring, you are well advised to observe how the handlers in the ring are conducting themselves.

the number of dogs in competition in each division (there are 14 divisions in all, based on geography) and may or may not change the numbers of dogs required for each number of points. For example, a major in Division 2 (Delaware, New Jersey and Pennsylvania) recently required 17 dogs or 16 bitches for a three-point major, 29 dogs or 27 bitches for a four-point major and 51 dogs or 46 bitches for a five-point major. The Great Pyrenees attracts fair numbers at all-breed shows, though not as many as the more common breeds.

Only one dog and one bitch of each breed can win points at a given show. There are no "co-ed" classes except for champions of record. Dogs and bitches do not compete against each other until they are champions. Dogs that are not champions (referred to as "class dogs") compete in one of five classes. The class in which a dog is entered depends on age and previous show wins. First, there is the Puppy Class (sometimes divided further into classes for 6- to 9-month-olds and 9- to 12-month-olds); next is the Novice Class (for dogs that have no points toward their championship and whose only first-place wins have come in the Puppy Class or the Novice Class, the latter class limited to three first places); then there is the American-bred Class (for dogs bred in the US); the

Bred-by-Exhibitor Class (for dogs handled by their breeders or by immediate family members of their breeders) and the Open Class (for any non-champions). Any dog may enter the Open class, regardless of age or win history, but, to be competitive, the dog should be older and have ring experience.

The judge at the show begins judging the dogs in the Puppy Classes and proceeds through the classes. The judge awards first through fourth place in each class. The first-place winners of each class then compete with one another in the Winners Class to determine Winners Dog. The judge then starts over with the bitches, beginning with the Puppy Classes and proceeding up to the Winners Class to award Winners

SEAL OF EXCELLENCE
The show ring is the testing ground for a breeder's program. A championship on a dog signifies that three qualified judges have placed their seal of approval on that dog. Only dogs that have earned their championships should be considered for breeding purposes. Striving to improve the breed and reproduce sound, typical examples of the breed, breeders must breed only the best. No breeder breeds only for pet homes; they strive for the top. The goal of every program must be to better the breed, and every responsible breeder wants the prestige of producing Best in Show winners.

Bitch, just as he did with the dogs. A Reserve Winners Dog and Reserve Winners Bitch are also selected; these could be awarded the points in the case of a disqualification.

The Winners Dog and Winners Bitch are the two that are awarded the points for their breed. They then go on to compete with any champions of record (often called "specials") of their breed that are entered in the show. The champions may be dogs or bitches; in this class, all are shown together. The judge reviews the Winners Dog and Winners Bitch along with all of the champions to select the Best of Breed winner. The Best of Winners is selected between the Winners Dog and Winners Bitch; if one of these two is selected Best of Breed as well, he or she is automatically determined Best of Winners. Lastly, the judge selects Best of Opposite Sex to the Best of Breed winner. The Best of Breed winner then goes on to the Group competition.

At a Group or all-breed show, the Best of Breed winners from each breed are divided into their respective groups to compete against one another for Group One through Group Four. Group One (first place) is awarded to the dog that best lives up to the ideal for his breed as described in the standard. A Group judge, therefore, must have a thorough

Pyreneans and their handlers in the breed ring, awaiting a look from the judge.

working knowledge of many breed standards. After placements have been made in each Group, the seven Group One winners (from the Sporting Group, Toy Group, Hound Group, etc.) compete against each other for the top honor, Best in Show.

Your Great Pyrenees must be six months of age or older and registered with the AKC in order to be entered in AKC-sanctioned shows in which there are classes for the Great Pyrenees. Your Great Pyrenees also must not possess any disqualifying faults and must be sexually intact. If you have spayed or neutered your dog, however, there are many AKC events other than conformation, such as obedience trials, agility trials and the Canine Good Citizen program, in which you and your Great Pyrenees can participate.

YOUR AGING

GREAT PYRENEES

When we bring home a puppy, full of the energy and exuberance that accompanies youth, we hope for a long, happy and fulfilling relationship with the new family member. Even when we adopt an older dog, we look forward to the years of companionship ahead with a new canine friend. However, aging is inevitable for all creatures, and there will come a time when our dog reaches his senior years and will need special consideration and attention to his care.

Changes in a senior dog can be rather subtle, especially on a white and gray dog, where the telltale graying muzzle will be difficult to detect.

WHEN IS MY DOG A "SENIOR"?

Dogs generally are considered "seniors" at seven years of age, but that is not always accurate. A dog's senior status is better determined based on the average life expectancy for his breed, which is based on the size of the breed. Average life expectancies are considered as follows: Small breeds, 12 years or more; medium breeds, 10 years or more; large breeds, 9 years or more and giant breeds, 7 years or more. A dog is considered a senior when he has reached 75% of the average lifespan for his breed. Your Great Pyrenees has an average lifespan of ten years, though some dogs only last to eight or nine.

Thus, the old "seven dog years to one human year" theory is not exact. In puppyhood, a dog's year is actually comparable to more than seven human years, considering the puppy's rapid growth during his first year. Then, in adulthood, the ratio decreases. Regardless, a more viable rule of thumb is that the larger the dog, the shorter his expected lifespan. Of course, this can vary among individual dogs, with many living longer than expected, which we hope is the case!

For the purposes of feeding and veterinary care, seven years is the age when most Great Pyrenees breeders consider the dog to be a senior.

WHAT ARE THE SIGNS OF AGING?

By the time your dog has reached his senior years, you will know him very well and, thus, the physical and behavioral changes that accompany aging should be noticeable to you. Humans and dogs share the most obvious physical sign of aging: gray hair! Graying often occurs first on the muzzle and face, around the eyes. Other telltale signs are the dog's overall decrease in activity. Your older dog might be more content to nap and rest, and he may not show the same old enthusiasm when it's time to play in the yard or go for a walk. Other physical signs include significant weight

Some Pyrs are lazy years before they're old!

CAUSES OF CHANGE

Cognitive dysfunction may not be the cause of all changes in your older dog; illness and medication can also affect him. Things like diabetes, Cushing's disease, cancer and brain tumors are serious physical problems but can cause behavioral changes as well. Older dogs are more prone to these conditions, so they should not be overlooked as possibilities for your dog's acting not like his "old self." Any significant changes in your senior's behavior are good reasons to take your dog to the vet for a thorough exam.

Your dog's reactions to medication can cause changes as well. The various types of corticosteroids are often cited as affecting a dog's behavior. If your vet prescribes any type of drug, discuss possible side effects before administering the medication to your old friend.

loss or gain; more labored movement; skin and coat problems, possibly hair loss; sight and/or hearing problems; changes in toileting habits, perhaps seeming "unhousebroken" at times; tooth decay, bad breath or other mouth problems.

There are behavioral changes that go along with aging, too. There are numerous causes for behavioral changes. Sometimes a dog's apparent confusion results from a physical change like

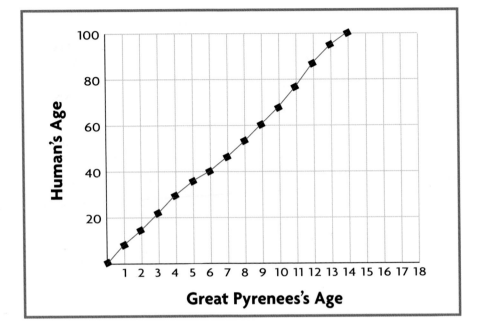

Great Pyrenees's Age

diminished sight or hearing. If his confusion causes him to be afraid, he may act aggressively or defensively. He may sleep more frequently because his daily walks, though shorter now, tire him out. He may begin to experience separation anxiety or, conversely, become less interested in petting and attention.

There also are clinical conditions that cause behavioral changes in older dog. One such condition is known as canine cognitive dysfunction (familiarly known as "old-dog" syndrome). It can be frustrating for an owner whose dog is affected with cognitive dysfunction, as it can result in behavioral changes of all

types, most seemingly unexplainable. Common changes include the dog's forgetting aspects of the daily routine, such as times to eat, go out for walks, relieve himself and the like. Along the same lines, you may take your dog out at the regular time for a potty trip and he may have no idea why he is there. Sometimes a placid dog will begin to show aggressive or possessive tendencies or, conversely, a hyperactive dog will start to "mellow out."

Disease also can be the cause of behavioral changes in senior dogs. Hormonal problems (Cushing's disease is common in older dogs), diabetes and thyroid disease can cause increased appetite, which can lead to aggression related to food guarding. It's better to be proactive with your senior dog, making more frequent trips to the vet if necessary and having bloodwork done to test for the diseases that can commonly befall older dogs.

This is not to say that as dogs age they all fall apart physically and become nasty in personality. The aforementioned changes are discussed to alert owners to the things that may happen as their dogs get older. Many hardy dogs remain active and alert well into old age. However, it can be frustrating and heartbreaking for owners to see their beloved dogs change physically and temperamentally. Just know that it's the same dog under there, and that he still loves you and appreciates your care, which he needs now more than ever.

HOW DO I CARE FOR MY AGING DOG?

Again, every dog is an individual in terms of aging. Your dog might reach the estimated "senior" age for his breed and show no signs of slowing down. However, even if he shows no outward signs of aging, he should begin a senior-care program once he reaches the determined age. He may not show it, but he's not a pup anymore! By providing him with extra attention to his veterinary care at this age, you will be practicing good

> **WEATHER WORRIES**
> Older pets are less tolerant of extremes in weather, both heat and cold. Your older dog should not spend extended periods in the sun; when outdoors in the warm weather, make sure he does not become overheated. In chilly weather, consider a sweater for your dog when outdoors and limit time spent outside. Whether or not his coat is thinning, he will need provisions to keep him warm when the weather is cold. You may even place his bed by a heating duct in your living room or bedroom.

preventative medicine, ensuring that the rest of your dog's life will be as long, active, happy and healthy as possible. If you do notice indications of aging, such as graying and/or changes in sleeping, eating or toileting habits, this is a sign to set up a senior-care visit with your vet right away to make sure that these changes are not related to any health problems.

To start, senior dogs should visit the vet twice yearly for exams, routine tests and overall evaluations. Many veterinarians have special screening programs especially for senior dogs that can include a thorough physical exam; blood test to determine complete blood count; serum biochemistry test, which screens for liver, kidney and blood problems as well as cancer; urinalysis; and dental exams. With these tests, it can be determined if your dog has any health problems; the results also establish a baseline for your pet against which future test results can be compared.

In addition to these tests, your vet may suggest additional testing, including an EKG, tests for glaucoma and other problems of the eye, chest X-rays, screening for tumors, blood pressure test, test for thyroid function and screening for parasites and reassessment of his preventative program. Your vet also will ask you questions about your dog's diet and activity level, what you feed and the amounts that you feed. This information, along with his evaluation of the dog's overall condition, will enable him to suggest proper dietary changes, if needed.

This may seem like quite a work-up for your pet, but veterinarians advise that older dogs need more frequent attention so that any health problems can be detected as early as possible. Serious conditions like kidney disease, heart disease and cancer may not present outward symptoms, or the problem may go undetected if the symptoms are mistaken by owners as just part of

Keep your senior dog in the best possible condition by adjusting his diet, exercise routine and the frequency of his veterinary visits.

the aging process.

There are some conditions more common in the elderly dogs that are difficult to ignore. Cognitive dysfunction shares much in common with senility and Alzheimer's disease, and dogs are not immune. Dogs can become confused and/or disoriented, lose their house-training, have abnormal sleep-wake cycles and interact differently with their owners. Be heartened by the fact that, in some ways, there are more treatment options for dogs with cognitive dysfunction than for people with similar conditions. There is good evidence that continued stimulation in the form of games, play, training and exercise can help to maintain cognitive function. There are also medications (such as seligiline) and antioxidant-fortified senior diets that have been shown to be beneficial.

Cancer is also a condition more common in the elderly. Almost all of the cancers seen in people are also seen in pets. While we can't control the effects of second-hand smoke, lung cancer, which is a major killer in humans, is relatively rare in dogs. If pets are getting regular physical examinations, cancers are often detected early. There are a variety of cancer therapies available today and many pets continue to live happy lives with appropriate treatment.

Degenerative joint disease, often referred to as arthritis, is another common malady shared between elderly dogs and humans. A lifetime of wear and tear on joints, and running around at play, eventually takes it toll and results in stiffness and difficulty getting around. As dogs live longer and healthier lives, it is natural that they should eventually feel some of the effects of aging. Once again, if regular veterinary care has been available, your pet was not carrying extra pounds all those years and wearing those joints out before their time. If your pet was unfortunate enough to inherit hip dysplasia, osteochondrosis dissecans, or any of the other developmental orthopedic diseases, battling the onset of degenerative joint disease was probably a longstanding goal. In any case, there are now many effective remedies for managing degenerative joint disease and a number of remarkable surgeries as well.

Aside from the extra veterinary care, there is much you can do at home to keep your older dog in good condition. The dog's diet is an important factor. If your dog's appetite decreases, he will not be getting the nutrients he needs. He also will lose weight, which is unhealthy for a dog at a proper weight. Conversely, an older dog's metabolism is slower and he usually exercises less, but he should not be allowed to become obese. Obesity in an older dog is especially risky, because extra pounds mean extra stress on the body, increasing his vulnerability to heart disease. Plus, the additional pounds make it harder for the dog to move about.

You should discuss age-related feeding changes with your vet. For a dog who has lost interest in food, it may be suggested to try some different types of food until you find something new that the dog likes. For an obese dog, a "light" formula dog food or

WHEN IS YOUR DOG A GERIATRIC?

A survey of the diplomates of the American Board of Veterinary Practicioners and the American Colleges of Veterinary Internal Medicine, Veterinary Surgery and Veterinary Pathologists defined a "geriatric" dog as one who begins to experience age-related health problems. The age at which to consider a dog geriatric is based on the dog's size. Small dogs, those that weigh 20 lbs or less, would be considered geriatric at around 12 years of age. Medium dogs, from 21 to 50 lbs, are geriatric at 10 years of age. Large dogs, from 51 to 90 lbs, at about 9 years of age. Giant dogs, those over 90 lbs, at about 8 years of age. These ages vary, of course, with individual dogs and breeds.

reducing food portions may be advised, along with exercise appropriate to his physical condition and energy level.

Keep up with your grooming routine as you always have. Be extra diligent about checking the skin and coat for problems. Older dogs can experience thinning coats as a normal aging process, but they can also lose hair as a result of medical problems. Some thinning is normal, but patches of baldness or the loss of significant amounts of hair is not.

Hopefully, you've been regular with brushing your dog's teeth throughout his life. Healthy teeth directly affect overall good health. We already know that bacteria from gum infections can enter the dog's body through the damaged gums and travel to the organs. At a stage in life when his organs don't function as well as they used to, you don't want anything to put additional strain on them. Clean teeth also contribute to a healthy immune system. Offering the dental-type chews in addition to toothbrushing can help, as they remove plaque and tartar as the dog chews.

Along with the same good care you've given him all of his life, pay a little extra attention to your dog in his senior years and keep up with twice-yearly trips to the vet. The sooner a problem is uncovered, the greater the chances of a full recovery.

INDEX

My Great Pyrenees

PUT YOUR PUPPY'S FIRST PICTURE HERE

Dog's Name _____

Date _____ Photographer _____